ORGANIZING

OPTIONS

ORGANIZING OPTIONS
is available from the
San Francisco Bay Area Chapter of the National
Association of Professional Organizers (NAPO)
1592 Union Street #721
San Francisco, CA 94123

CONTRIBUTORS

This book could never have been published without the generous financial and consulting support of the following people and organizations. To all of you we offer our heartfelt thanks for your faith in us and the value of the work that we do.

Theo Gund
(Formerly our Anonymous Angel.
Bless you!)

Rossow Resources
Lillian Vernon Corporation
FlexAddress® Systems

Ducks in a Row, Fay Giordano

Wayne Wilson, Consulting
(Custom Databases & General Macintosh® Consulting,
San Rafael, California)

Harold Taylor Time Consultants, Inc.

Donations in Memory of Mary Mead Lynch
Mary Rossow
Pamela Small-Austin
Mrs. Elizabeth Mead
Beth Blair

ORGANIZING OPTIONS

Solutions from Professional Organizers

by the

**San Francisco
Bay Area Chapter
Members**

of the

**National
Association of
Professional Organizers
(NAPO)**

IF I COULD JUST GET ORGANIZED
Author unknown

There may be nothing wrong with you,
The way you live, the work you do.
But I can very plainly see
Exactly what is wrong with me.

It isn't that I'm indolent
Or dodging duty by intent.
I work as hard as anyone
And still I get so little done.

I nibble this, I nibble that,
But never finish what I'm at.

The morning goes, the noon is near.
Before I know the night is here.
And all around me I regret
The things I haven't finished yet.

I nibble this, I nibble that,
But never finish what I'm at.

I often times have realized
Not all that matters is the man.
The man must also have a plan.
I'd do so much—you'd be surprised—
If I could just get organized.

EDITOR'S PREFACE

The original idea for this book came from former San Francisco Bay Area NAPO Chapter president Anacaria Myrrha, some of whose excellent writing appears in the following pages. Her original vision was of a *booklet* of organizing tips, which we chapter members could use to make the public more aware of our relatively new profession, and to promote ourselves.

At a chapter board of directors' retreat in August 1991, board members Karen Magorian, Leslie Martin, Anacaria Myrrha, Annie Rohrbach and Arleen Westcott spent time developing the concept and later presented it to the chapter membership for acceptance and input.

In December 1991, myself a relatively new member of NAPO, I agreed to serve as project director for the Tips Book*let*. Little did I know what I was taking on! The project officially began at our February 1992 chapter meeting, and within a very short time it became clear that our little booklet was destined to be a full-fledged book.

What you are holding in your hand is the product of thousands of hours work by many dedicated volunteers —all members of NAPO. The Bay Area Chapter members take pride in the spirit of cooperation that permeates our organization, and this book is a shining testimony to that cooperative spirit. I am privileged to know all these fine men and women as colleagues and friends. I hope you will take advantage of the opportunity to know some of them yourselves through the membership directory at the end of the book.

Some brief comments about what you will find here:

We do not pretend that this book is the be-all and end-all of comprehensive books about organizing. We do believe that the information we offer is high quality and will serve you well when you take contributors' suggestions to heart.

We have arranged information alphabetically by categories for simplicity's sake and done our best to put information in logical places.

In the interest of political correctness, gender balance, and to avoid stylistic awkwardness, we have elected to mix the use of masculine and feminine pronouns.

The focus of the book is deliberately general and covers a broad range of home, office and personal management topics. The material represents the full spectrum of skills and specialties of our members.

You will find that some information overlaps. There may be more than one solution suggested for the same problem, and sometimes different solutions may seem to contradict one another. There is a very good reason for this: There is no "one best way" for everyone. Each situation is unique, and as professional organizers, we all approach every client challenge with that in mind. One person's solution may not work for you; another's may work like a charm. The proof is always "in the pudding," as my grandmother used to say, and that's why we've given you *Options*.

Happy Organizing!

Diana Dring
Executive Editor

ACKNOWLEDGMENTS

Practically every Bay Area NAPO Chapter member has contributed something to this book; yet there are some people who deserve special thanks, for without their selfless dedication, none of this would have been possible.

Anacaria Myrrha, for conceiving the project, for her continuous moral support throughout every stage of its development, and for her companionship, patience and acute sense of style in the final hours of editing and preparing this manuscript for press.

Karen Magorian, Leslie Martin, Anacaria Myrrha, Annie Rohrbach and **Arleen Westcott,** 1991 chapter board of directors members, for original concept development.

Lee Victoria Larsen, Art Director and Development Committee Chair, for being one of the Executive Editor's two extra right arms. Her dedication to the completion of this project went far beyond the call of duty. Her vision and diplomacy, as well as her masterful scheduling and management of committee meeting agenda, kept us productive and focused. Her attention to the details of design and printing are largely responsible for the high quality of our graphic presentation. The value of her contribution is beyond measure.

Annie Rohrbach, Directory Editor, for being the Executive Editor's other extra right arm through thick and thin and thick again. Annie's creativity, ingenuity, attention to detail, perseverance, humor and compassion for late-comers have made both the main directory and the superb chart of services at the back of this book the outstanding resource it is. Words cannot express the importance of her contribution!

Karen Magorian, Finance Manager, for so competently and conscientiously managing our fund raising and cash flow.

Beth Blair, Associate Editor, for her original content edit, perceptive suggestions and moral support during a particularly trying time.

Hester Lox, Copy Editor, for undertaking the mammoth job of translating the first draft into good English with style and wit!

Carol Kampe, Managing Editor, for the generous loan of her computer and her nimble fingers for the original manuscript input. Thanks also to **Jafra Austin** for original computer input.

Tudi Baskay, Development Committee member, for sorting and organizing all the original articles and tips submitted by members so they could be input to the computer—and for her humor, tenacity and critical eye.

Eve Abbott, Judy DeVivo, Karen Larsen, Karen Rossum and **Gretchen Schomp,** for their time and computers to input additional material.

Sue Barrera, Tudi Baskay, Marsha Freid, Laura Higgins, Celeste Lane, Keven Madvig, Gretchen Schomp and **Angela Wallace**, for their sharp eyes in the proofreading process.

Arnold Chasinov, Development Committee member, for graphic arts research, moral support, and for compiling the recommended reading list.

Barbara Raleigh, Development Committee member, for coming up with the winning title, and for her attention to detail.

Priscilla Carvalho, Distribution Manager, for managing the distribution plan.

Mary Rossow, for her fun(d) raising expertise and great contacts.

Leslie Martin, for her invaluable computer expertise.

Linda Lipton, for her wonderful cover design.

... and to all the other chapter members who have participated in the birthing of this book, **thank you for your support!**

Diana Dring
Executive Editor

A
SPECIAL
ACKNOWLEDGMENT

The Board of Directors and general membership of the Bay Area Chapter of NAPO wish to acknowledge our **Executive Editor, Diana Dring.** Drawing on her extensive background in editing and publishing, as well as her strong organizational skills, she spearheaded the strategic planning for this book and guided various committees through financing, editing, design and distribution. We honor Diana for her gifts, her fortitude and persistence, her sense of humor, her honesty, her ability to ask for help, and for her knowledge of professional editing and the publication process. We are proud of what we have produced, and we are deeply grateful to Diana for directing us throughout this project.

TABLE OF CONTENTS

I. Introduction

II. Tips from Professional Organizers

TABLE OF CONTENTS, continued

I

INTRODUCTION

"Organizing is what you do before you do something, so that when you do it, it's not all mixed up."

— A.A. Milne

ORGANIZATION:
THE JOURNEY OF A LIFETIME!

Being organized means having dependable systems for keeping track of things. Dependable systems give you reliable access to information, products and possessions. Knowing that you can find what you need when you need it gives you a feeling of security and enables you to function with a high degree of creativity, productivity and effectiveness.

Modern dictionaries define organization as the systematic grouping of things into logical relationships, types, or sequences. To organize means to arrange things in a way that creates a harmonious, unified structure of the whole—which, in turn, increases our ability to function effectively within the structures and circumstances of our lives.

If we rely solely on the dictionary definition, however, we may be tempted to think of getting organized as reaching a goal which, once accomplished, is "finished" and complete. On the contrary, creating order—and maintaining it—is not a destination but a journey; not a goal but a process. There is no finish line. There is only the process of becoming, and the present moment of our progress on that journey.

Because we live in a society that is predominantly goal-oriented, many of us have not learned to live in a process-oriented way. We have been taught that if we can just get things figured out, organized and under control, we will "arrive," we will have succeeded. But somehow, we never seem to get to the endpoint; there is always something else to do. This accounts for much of the frustration and sense of futility many people feel in the process of getting organized—and why, too often, the task seems overwhelming, and we are tempted to give up.

If we can accept the concept of organization as a process and view our days from this perspective, we can learn to relax, avoid much of the frustration that comes with our impatience for completion, and be comfortable with today. We can acknowledge and credit ourselves for the progress we *do* make, and let any unfinished business wait for tomorrow. We can come into harmony with the way things are.

Accepting organization as a process does not mean abdicating responsibility for setting limits. It does mean drawing boundaries and making choices in order to create effective systems. It means having a plan—and the better the plan, the more carefully we think through our needs and our purpose, the better the systems we create will function.

What stops many people from embarking on the process of getting organized is the notion that there is a right way to do it. Getting organized is about finding the ways and creating the systems that work for *you*. There's no right or wrong way to

2

organize things *your* way. And the best advice anyone may ever give you is: Keep It Simple, Sweetie (KISS).

As you embark on your own journey of better organization, the following simple guidelines will be useful to remember:

Being organized is not a moral issue. If you have a messy desk, untidy closets and drawers, and you don't show up on time, it is not an indication that you are a person of inferior character. You may never have learned how to put things in order, you may never have taken the time to do so, or you may have more to do than you can possibly do.

Perfectionism is a waste of time. To strive for excellence is recommended, particularly in important areas. But in ordinary daily transactions with components of a transitory nature, go for "ordinary best."

"Handle it once" is an unrealistic and anxiety producing concept. It is only possible if you take something out of your mailbox and immediately throw it away or send it to someone else's mailbox. "Handle it once at each step of its process" is realistic and appropriate.

Be willing to be flexible. Different times and conditions require different methods and procedures. Organize things the way they work best for you and set some policies as a basis for daily operations. However, when systems or procedures become difficult or cumbersome, take the time and make the decisions necessary to correct your course.

Don't be afraid to ask for help. When you are starting the process of becoming better organized, letting go of clutter and your attachments can be difficult and painful. The process will be easier if you do not do it alone. Consider asking a trusted friend, family member or organizing professional to offer support and help keep you focused.

IF YOUR LIFE IS DISORGANIZED, TREAT YOURSELF GENTLY !

Annie Rohrbach

When I ask people what they need to organize, they often say "my life!" They often feel embarrassed and find it hard to ask for help. They can be very critical of themselves. They may feel hopelessly overwhelmed, and have no concept of how or where to start. I have found that a transformation can occur much more easily if there is a change in attitude and in the way we choose to treat ourselves.

When I begin working with clients, especially if there is a lot of work to do, I often suggest that they measure their progress in terms of percentages. For example, once something is in its proper place, putting it back there 10% of the time is a measurable step forward from rarely putting it back at all—it's a move in the right direction. And when that behavior starts to become automatic, it is cause for real celebration! I therefore suggest to my clients that they give themselves credit all along the way for whatever progress they are making, and that they honor and acknowledge their achievements.

I also encourage my clients to become more aware of the negative messages they give themselves (often dozens of times each day) about being messy or disorganized or forgetful or bad, when they can't find something or finish something, or when they find themselves scowling at the piles and layers of their papers and possessions. I suggest they replace that negative self-talk with phrases like "I am becoming more organized," "I am taking care of this" or "I know where this goes." I will listen for comments from clients as I work with them, and when they express feelings of satisfaction and progress, I ask them to "say that again." Clients then learn to recognize and create their own good messages, which in turn make them feel much better.

Positive self-talk produces better results. People are more willing to change their habits and behaviors if they are encouraged and praised rather than criticized and punished. I suggest that my clients pay attention to the behaviors they desire and try to ignore the old behaviors and habits they are getting rid of. My clients find that their progress and the change in their rate of success will sometimes move very slowly and at other times very quickly. They cannot expect to go from disorganized to totally organized (black to white) in a short period of time. Therefore, I suggest that they concentrate more on the gray areas in between.

No one can expect to change and create new behaviors and habits overnight. If there are many new habits to create, and if one wishes to make a thorough and permanent transformation, it takes time. Once you understand this, you'll feel much better about yourself, give yourself credit for moving in the right direction, and recognize more quickly that you are indeed making progress. Treat yourself gently, with kindness, love and compassion. It can be magical. It can create dramatic changes, and it can lead to a more organized, balanced and happier life.

SOME SPECIFIC BENEFITS
OF BEING ORGANIZED

Confidence

Consistency

Dependable Systems

Easier Maintenance

Easier Retrieval of Information

Increased Creativity

Increased Effectiveness

Increased Productivity

More Aesthetically Pleasing Environment

Peace of Mind

Reduced Stress

Reliable Access to Possessions

Relief from Anxiety

Sense of Security

Time Savings

WHAT IS A PROFESSIONAL ORGANIZER?

Tudi Baskay

The concept of "Professional Organizer" is new to most people. The notion that there are people out there whose entire careers are dedicated to helping others get organized still raises eyebrows. Yet, those of us who have chosen to earn our living this way are blessed with a personal talent that brings us many rewards. Our talent is the ability to see the relationships of things to each other. Our passion is for having things arranged logically and running smoothly. Our joy is helping people bring order into their lives and seeing the difference that it makes for them in productivity, ease and satisfaction.

The basic mission of a professional organizer is to assist clients to set up and maintain good systems for managing the stuff of life—whatever that may be. Typically, chaotic environments result because people lack the time and tools they need to understand the causes of jumble and to deal with it. A professional organizer is a person who can analyze a chaotic situation, identify its sources, and then either suggest or design and implement a solution.

Equally important, a professional organizer's very presence is usually enough to help a client focus on an organization problem. That in itself starts the process of clarification, which eventually will lead to the discovery of a solution. A professional organizer creates an oasis where there is time to think about what the problem really is, what caused it, and what resources are available to solve it. Once a problem's cause is identified, a professional organizer brings to the situation her knowledge of methods and a fresh perspective, which enable the client and organizer together to design an appropriate solution that will prevent the problem from recurring.

7

Anacaria Myrrha, past president of the San Francisco Chapter of NAPO, characterized the "professional organizer's gift" quite eloquently in an article by the same title:

"In the midst of turbulent times, the Professional Organizer has a great gift to offer. To begin with, we take time to listen. When we begin to understand the problems, we question the status quo. We ask, 'how can this be done differently in order to effect a more desirable result?' We then engage in practical creative problem solving. We provide our clients with blueprints for harmonious environments. We offer techniques to improve their quality of life. We blend beauty with practicality. And most important of all, we offer non-judgmental support through the changes. There is no special magic to this process; just a lot of hard work done with wise intelligence and an open heart."

There are many reasons why people call on professional organizers for help. The trigger can be a storage problem that's gotten out of control, poor self-management habits that are negatively affecting business or personal productivity, a project that's too large for regular staff people to deal with in addition to their normal workload, new employees who need to be assimilated into a workflow system, or any one of many others.

The range of specialization and expertise among professional organizers is as varied as there are reasons why people seek them out. Some organizers specialize in organizing homes, some in offices. Some focus on specific rooms of the home (garages, kitchens or libraries) or aspects of office work (filing systems, procedures manuals, computers). Some organizers concentrate on managing projects and events, some in managing space. Others focus on less tangible areas such as setting goals, managing time and maintaining personal balance. Whatever the need, there is a professional organizer with the expertise to assist, train or coach you toward higher levels of productivity and effectiveness.

8

The National Association of Professional Organizers (NAPO) was founded in 1985 by six professional organizers working independently in California. The association now has 654 members and six active chapters throughout the U.S., as well as members in American Samoa, Canada, Germany and New Zealand. At this writing, the San Francisco Bay Area Chapter is NAPO's largest and most active branch with more than 100 members whose services span the full range of organizing specialties. (See the Directory of NAPO members at the back of this book.)

WHEN IS IT TIME TO CALL IN A PRO?
Laura Higgins

We are taught early and well how to accumulate stuff. We get presents for holidays and life-cycle events, like birthdays. So we go through life sitting on a pile that grows bigger and bigger, *taking* more *from* us. The more stuff you have, the more you have to store, clean, insure, keep track of, move. Pick up any book on organizing and the litany goes: Simplify! Reduce! Divest! But how?

You know you need the help of a professional organizer when you seem to spend more time feeling frazzled than you do having fun and being productive—when you dread the coming morning because it brings more chaos, more running behind the clock—when you haven't a clue how to improve such a situation; or you do have a clue, but the prospect of doing it all yourself is just too daunting. You need the help of a professional organizer when you have a major life change looming and not enough hours in the day to prepare for it.

Call a Pro and Save Your Sanity When:

- you're planning to move, or you think you need to move because you're out of storage space.
- you're starting a home-based business, or the one you have appears to be outgrowing its bounds.
- you're having a baby, and need to carve out space for a nursery.
- you're not prepared for earthquake, fire or other calamity—e.g., you can't find your insurance policy, don't have a home inventory.
- your mother is coming to live with you.
- you can never find infrequently-used items.
- you have house guests coming and want to create extra temporary space so they will be comfortable.
- you're getting married or divorced.
- you're going back to school.
- you're redecorating.
- you have some new hobbies.
- you need to create a home filing system.
- you want to sort your memorabilia.
- you have to prepare your home for sale.
- you want to organize a home improvement project and don't know where to start.
- you'd love to blast through those nagging "want to do" lists—the ones you never have time to put on your real "to do" list.
- you recognize that the system you've been using to cope with any of the above has not been working.

WORKING WITH A CONSULTANT
Leslie K. Martin

Most of us have, at one time or another, hired someone to provide a service for us. Hiring a contractor or an independent consultant always involves inherent risk for both parties. As

10

with any relationship, the basis of a harmonious one between client and consultant is shared effort and communication.

When hiring a consultant or contractor, there are some obvious initial steps to take. Start by asking good friends whose judgment you trust whether they have ever had similar work done, what their experiences were, and whether they would recommend the consultant/firm that did the work.

A business license can be a good sign that a person is serious about her commitment to her trade. It generally means she believes she is going to be in town long enough to want to be on the good side of city requirements, that she has some basic qualifications, and that she plans on paying taxes in her community.

Find out how long the company has been in business. You may want to call the Better Business Bureau, but my experience with the bureau is that its information about particular companies is limited and superficial.

Instead ask the contractor for references and then *call* the references. Ask to see samples or pictures of past work. Find out what the consultant's particular specialty or area of knowledge is. If it doesn't match your need, ask for a referral or ask how the consultant would handle the situation.

In the past, when I have hired someone, I have been in one of three frames of mind:

1.   I need a job done, and I just want somebody to come over and do it for me.

2.   I have an idealistic vision of what the end result should be. I have very definite ideas of what is supposed to happen, and I hover nervously and bite my nails through each step of the process.

11

3.   I have an idea of what I want, but I am not certain of the specific options available or necessary detail work required, so I present my idea and ask for guidance from the professional I've contacted.

From a consultant's perspective, obviously the first and third options are the most desirable. The first is a nice bread-and-butter job, but it won't provide the personal satisfaction, teamwork and appreciation that job number three has to offer. Job number two is often the job that I knew was going to be a nightmare, the one that I wish I had trusted my instinct to decline.

How to Prepare Yourself to Work with a Contractor

1.   **Do some homework.** You aren't expected to know the ins and outs of the trade or to be aware of the latest trends and improvements in the field. But spending a couple of hours at the local library or a bookstore reading up on the subject will make it easier to communicate what you expect your consultant to do for you. Your consultant can then provide the education, background and details needed to realize your vision. She'll find the best way to get as close as she can to fulfilling your dream within your budget.

2.   **Agree on what will be done.** This seems like simple common sense, but often I have thought I was hiring someone to do a particular job only to find out part-way through that what I really needed or wanted was something else. As a contractor I know how crucial it is to be certain I understand what is required. It's unfair to hold a consultant accountable for a client's inner feelings and needs that were never clearly expressed. Writing out a prioritized list before you sit down with your consultant will give both of you a path to follow. If you're in doubt, ask your consultant to tell you what he believes are the most important issues and see if you agree.

3.   **Specify payment terms up front.** A good contractor will tell you her terms before commencing work. Don't allow yourself to

be surprised by not getting a quote at the beginning. Some consultants will require a down payment. Some will ask for one third up front, one third midway through the job and one third at its conclusion. Nearly all will require payment in full upon completion; occasionally a payment plan may be acceptable. Whatever your agreement, put it in writing, signed by both parties, at the onset.

4. Agree on some part-way checkpoints where you will evaluate together the job's progress and make certain the project is on track.

5. Allow the contractor to do her job. Keep in mind that you're paying a specialist's price, so remember to listen to your consultant's advice and suggestions. Be open to her expertise and experience.

6. If possible, don't change your mind in mid-stream. If you do, know that it will cost you. There's no easy way around this one. That's why it's so crucial to clarify up front what you want and expect. If the contractor has to rip up what's been done and start over, expenses must be refigured, schedules must be changed and the whole process restarted—all of which takes time, which equals money.

7. Be there for job completion. Now is the time to take a comprehensive look and have any final adjustments made. It's easier and much nicer for both sides to view the finished product and discuss the outcome together. It's as much a genuine pleasure to do something of value for another as it is terrific to have a vision brought to life.

NINE STEPS TO ORGANIZATION
Anacaria Myrrha

When you made your New Year's resolutions last January, was "Get organized!" near the top of your list? Did you make the same resolution last year? And the year before? Is your desk still stacked with magazines, catalogues, event schedules, junk mail and very important things to do? Are your closets still untidy and your photos stuffed in shoe boxes? Does your garage make you think that a bulldozer may be the only answer? Do you feel like you will never find the time to do the things you love to do?

Perhaps you are feeling that there is something wrong with you because you just can't seem to get organized. You ought to be able to do it yourself. Right? Not necessarily. It is very likely that no one ever taught you how to get organized. Our parents and grandparents were not faced with the paper onslaught of the current information age, and schools did not address it in their curricula. Even now, with all the excellent organizing books available, the task of getting organized may seem overwhelming.

Don't despair. You *can* create order in your life. Here are nine steps you can take to get you started. The first four deal with internal attitudes and address your willingness to make the necessary commitments. The next four involve external components which provide a format for creating systems. The last, but not the least, is where you can go for help.

Attitudes

1. Time. To begin, you must be willing to commit the necessary time and attention to set up the systems. However many hours it takes, this investment will save you hundreds of hours (and a lot of anxiety) in the future. How long it takes will depend on the size of the task and the number of hours you can devote on any given day. Basic paper and workflow systems can usually be set up in a day, small filing systems in a week. Large filing systems take longer. Projects, like photo albums or travel files, can be gathered in boxes and worked on one at a time, a method that helps defuse the sense of overwhelm. Once a system is in use, refinements and modifications can be made as necessary.

2. Decisions. Next, you must be willing to make the necessary decisions to set up the systems. If you turn the design over to someone else, you will wind up with a system that works for them but not necessarily for you. Your systems need to be created with attention to your particular priorities, patterns and style.

3. Change. You must also be willing to embrace new habits. If you find yourself saying, "That's the way I've always done it," or, "I've always been disorganized, unfocused, late, . . ." try a new approach. Begin to say, "I used to be disorganized, unfocused and late, but now I'm organized, focused, and on time." Positive speaking, like positive thinking, is a very powerful tool and can be used to your advantage. With this approach, and the support of systems designed with ease of use as a factor, the transition to new habits can be easy.

4. Maintenance. Because being organized is a process and not a goal, you must be willing to commit regular time to maintain your systems. This is the one we often put off because we are taking care of what seem to be more urgent tasks. However, when chaos piles up, the simplest tasks become difficult and time consuming as we search for bills to pay or our child's school authorization form. With the constant flow of information and paper in our lives, and our changing personal and professional needs, it is crucial to schedule regular time to plan, to file, and to update systems.

Components of Organization

5. Containers. One reason disorder occurs is the lack of boundaries. Without boundaries, paper piles spill onto other paper piles. Pens and pencils, rubber bands and paper clips become a jumble in desk drawers. Children's toys, kitchen utensils, tools and hardware become mixed together and are time consuming and annoying to retrieve. A container is the first step in the solution. A container sets limits on the space the items inhabit and keeps them in their place.

Containers come in all shapes and sizes. File folders, file cabinets and desk racks contain papers. Drawers and drawer organizers contain tools. Planning notebooks contain appointments, tasks and resources. Even an increment of time can be viewed as a container (a task scheduled from 1:00 to 3:00 on Tuesday afternoon can be comfortably set aside until its time arrives). Magazine boxes and shelves, scrapbooks and photo albums all act as containers to set boundaries for objects and information, and help to create order in our lives.

6. Labels. The second component is the right label on a container. This label tells you (and others) what belongs in the container. More important, it tells you (and others) what does *not* belong in the container.

7. Procedures. A procedure should be thought out for getting things into and out of each container. If the procedure has several steps, it can be written down on a card and attached to the container. For instance, the procedures for filing health insurance claims can be taped to the front of a vertical file rack containing file folders of claims in their various stages of completion.

8. Location. If you have old IRS records in your desk drawers and resource information for a current project in a file cabinet with your ski equipment stacked in front of it, your project work will be difficult and your anxiety level high. Put the IRS records in labeled, uniform-size storage boxes in the closet and hang the skis in the garage. Place your Current Projects and Action Files in a desk file drawer or in a vertical rack on your work surface. Also, keep all the necessary tools for particular tasks in the area where the work is done.

Asking for Help

9. The Professional Organizer. Most of us have mechanics to doctor our cars, accountants to prepare our tax returns, lawyers to negotiate our contracts, and housekeepers to tidy our nests. However, it is often difficult for us to ask for help with a task about which we feel out of control, embarrassed, or that we ought to be able to do ourselves. Remember, being organized is not a moral issue. It is a skill that can be learned. The good news is, help is available. You can now hire a professional organizer to help you learn that skill. A professional organizer can offer creative problem solving and an objective view, provide you with practical solutions, and support you and keep you on track during the process of change.

THE BASICS OF SPACE PLANNING
Annie Rohrbach

When trying to decide what goes where, from the largest piece of furniture to the smallest box or paper clip, first decide how you are going to use each space. What is it for? What are you going to do there? What do you need in order to do those things?

How much storage is needed for immediate use, moderate use, occasional use? Anything used frequently should be easily accessible. Items used infrequently can be placed higher, lower, behind or out of sight. The more you use something the more conveniently it needs to be placed. This rule of thumb is especially important when planning your kitchen, your office or your desk space. Place the things you need in the area where you are going to use them.

For example, at the kitchen sink you will obviously need soaps, brushes, sponges and dish drainer, but how about the cutting

17

knives and cutting boards, vegetable peeler, colander, can opener and trash container? Likewise, keep containers for leftovers near the refrigerator (together with their lids), plus foil, plastic wrap, baggies and other supplies you use to store leftovers.

QUEEN OF INFINITE SPACE

Tudi Baskay

If all my walls were rubber
And all my drawers were deep,
Just think of all the gadgets
That I'd have space to keep.

The books I've got in boxes
I'd push against the wall,
And with a wall of rubber
I'd use no space at all.

That dress I liked last summer,
The shoes that don't quite fit,
The purse I broke the strap on:
I'd get to keep each bit.

Out in my kitchen cabinet
(And on the pantry shelf)
There'd be a thousand products
I'll never use myself.

Old letters, bills, and recipes
I always meant to try—
Old magazines and flyers:
In one deep drawer they'd lie.

If all my walls were rubber
And all my drawers were deep,
I'd never find a single thing
Among the things I'd keep.

II

ORGANIZING TIPS

from

San Francisco
Bay Area Chapter
Members

of the

National
Association of
Professional Organizers

(NAPO)

1
AUTOMOBILES

"She can't keep much trash in a Mustang, and that's what she likes. Travel light. Don't keep what does not have immediate uses. The road thinks ahead."

— Louise Erdrich,
The Lady in the Pink Mustang

ORGANIZING YOUR VEHICLE
Annie Rohrbach

If you make a point of keeping your car organized and clean inside and out, it can decrease your stress level, and you will feel better every time you get in and out of you car. This process can also inspire you to keep other environments more organized and cleaner.

Keep your car neater by using containers to hold such things as papers to photocopy, film and other items to drop off or deliver to others, receipts, notes and other papers that accumulate while doing errands, dry cleaning, etc. Other containers for snacks, water, tissues, and disaster preparedness supplies are also important.

KEEPING BUSINESS LITERATURE UNDER CONTROL ON THE ROAD

Barbara Raleigh

Problem: When meeting with clients, do you sometimes find that you do not have the literature you need with you? Or, to make sure that you always have what you need, do you carry every brochure you could conceivably ever need, and are they strewn all over the trunk or back seat of your vehicle, or jammed in your briefcase?

Solution: Buy a storage bin in which you can suspend hanging files. Make a separate file for each piece of literature. Put the hanging files in alphabetical order (with sub-files inserted if you so choose). Schedule a regular weekly time to restock your supplies.

Problem: Do you travel extensively and have maps, tour books and the like all over the trunk of your vehicle?

Solution: Follow the instructions above, but label the files for various cities, states or regional areas. State files can subdivided into cities or counties. Alternatively, buy an expanding envelope with 30 sections. Label each section by city, state or other appropriate area. (Note: an expansion envelope will neither hold as much as a storage bin, nor be as sturdy.)

BASIC SUPPLIES TO KEEP IN YOUR CAR
Beth Blair

Clean rags and towelettes
Coins (quarters, dimes)
Collapsible tote bag or backpack
Comfortable walking shoes and socks
Extra batteries for radio and flashlight
First aid kit(an old lunch box is useful)
Flares
Flashlight
Jacket
Jumper Cables
List of emergency phone numbers (AAA, tow service, repair
shop, relatives, child care providers, neighbors)
Map book/maps of your area
Mending kit
Menstrual supplies
Non-perishable food (granola bars, dried fruit, etc.)
Sealed bottled drinking water
Pens/paper
Personal medications
Plastic rain poncho
Pocket knife (Swiss Army style)
Portable radio
Safety pins
Sleeping bag or survival blanket
Work gloves
Tissues and/or toilet paper
Waterproof matches (for flares)
Work gloves

To contain these items, consider using a strong plastic bin with a
snap-on lid, a small square laundry basket, a duffel bag made of
rip-stop nylon or heavy cotton, or a collapsible crate. Food and
water could be kept in a plastic shoe-size box with a snap-on
lid.

MORE TIPS

✦ Use a small, square laundry basket in the front seat of your car to collect all receipts, purchases, school forms, etc., gathered during the day. It allows you to keep your car tidy and get everything into the house with fewer trips between house and automobile.

✦ Keep baby wipes in the glove box of your car. They are great for cleaning your hands after pumping gas, washing sticky children, removing food crumbs from the upholstery, and wiping up food spills.

✦ If you live in a metropolitan area, you may shop in many surrounding communities at stores that carry items not available in your neighborhood, or where there are better prices and a wider selection of merchandise.

Carry a small spiral notebook in your car. When you think of something that you need from an outlying store, title a page with the name of the community and make a note of the item you want to buy. As you think of other things you need, add them to the list. Use the same notebook to jot down names and addresses of businesses you've heard about, restaurants you've been meaning to try, or other points of interest.

When the list gets long enough to warrant a special trip, or the next time you're in that area, you'll have your shopping list with you. With this system you avoid having to ask yourself that awful question: "Oh, why didn't I remember?" and you save time and mileage on out-of-town shopping trips.

✦ Carry a getaway kit (a small, plastic-lined nylon bag with basic toiletries and cosmetics) in the trunk of the car . If you have an unexpected invitation or simply want to freshen up, your own soap, toothbrush, toothpaste and complete makeup kit are available to you.

✦ Use a clean blackboard eraser to wipe off the condensation from inside car windows. Children like to help with this and it helps keep their grubby fingers off the windows. Keep the eraser in the glove compartment.

2
BALANCE

"All intellectual improvement arises from leisure."

— Samuel Johnson

ACHIEVING A BALANCED LIFE
Annie Rohrbach

Part of the process of becoming more organized involves making a commitment to achieve more balance in your life. The more balanced life is, the less complicated it becomes. We feel less stressed. We feel better about ourselves. We learn to replace the "I shoulds" in our lives with "I want to" or "I choose to." We have more choices. We can eliminate that which is not important to us and have more time for that which *is* important. We can then more easily focus on our priorities. When we are doing things that are more meaningful to us and that we really enjoy, we are not as likely to put things off. In fact, we look forward to what we do. Instead of feeling that our lives control us, we feel in control of our lives.

So how do we achieve that balance? The best way I know is to go through an exploratory process. Write down the kinds of things you do that you enjoy and that you want to have more of in your life. What do you need? What do you *not* need? How do you spend your time? How do you *want* to spend your time? Do you spend too much time in some areas and not enough in others?

29

Once you have explored this, try to group the things you have discovered into categories. Here are some possibilities:

work-play	self-others
indoors-outdoors	keeping-letting go
active-quiet	spouse-kids
mountains-ocean	left brain-right brain
mind-body	friends-family
warm-cold	linear-circular
order-chaos	giving-taking
casual-dressy	scattered-centered
clean-dirty	laughter-tears
spending-saving	imbalance-balanced

When you determine the categories that work for you, take a look at each one and decide what balance means to you. For example, do you feel best when you can spend 20% of your time outdoors and 80% indoors, or is it the other way around? Your personal degree of balance does not have to be 50-50. Be sure to factor in what you would like it to be as well as what is realistic.

As you work to achieve greater balance for yourself, you may want to work on just one or two areas of your life at a time, adding more as you are ready. You may want to monitor your progress on a daily basis (one day at a time) or track yourself weekly, monthly or even yearly. As your life and your goals change, go back and redefine and adjust your balance factors accordingly. Knowing you do best when more areas of your life are in balance, you can then make the necessary adjustments in your plans and your schedule and so that your life is back in balance again.

This process can help you to be more selective about what you choose to do and not do, to set boundaries, to plan your time, and to decide on both short-term and long-term goals. You can use it to evaluate how you are doing and what you might want to do differently.

It has been my experience that going through this process leads us to become more organized and make our lives less complicated. We feel less stress, and we feel much better about ourselves and the way we live. It also provides us with a way to validate, honor and acknowledge the work we do.

From the Lillian Vernon Catalog

3

CASH

MANAGEMENT

"Money is flat and meant to be piled up."

— Scottish Proverb

FOUR EASY STEPS TO A
CASH MANAGEMENT PLAN

Lee Victoria Larsen

Decisions about handling money are one of the most persistent challenges in our daily lives. For most people, cash management is learned by default. We somehow expect that we should each be masterful at managing our money, yet good cash management results from learned skills.

The first step for setting up your cash management system must be to write down your goals.

Here are four easy steps for setting up your cash management:

Step 1. First, put your calculator away! To design a cash management system that works, you must base it on your own passions and priorities. Begin by making a quick list of what's most important to you. Then expand the list to include your priorities in professional, personal, family, relationship, financial, physical, spiritual/religious, health, recreation and community areas.

This forms a template from which you can begin changing old habits to open up a new possibilities that are meaningful and exciting. For example: if you have just discovered a new spark of joy from making a commitment to trekking in the Amazon in two years, then you can harness this desire to begin regular saving to make the dream a reality. To accomplish it, you'll need to earn more or spend less. Either way, you will need to change old habits, and this is a significant feat. Focus on what you *really* want so that you can change habits. By reading your goals daily or weekly and remembering what you really want, you can start making new choices.

Step 2. Set up a daily, monthly and quarterly routine. Determine whether you need a bare-bones pencil and paper system or a computer and software to implement your plan. Choose whatever seems easiest to you. A tip: if doing Step 3 exceeds the suggested time frames, it is worthwhile to consider switching to a computer to save your valuable time.

Step 3. Schedule actual appointments onto your calendar for cash management tasks. For example:

- First Week: Reconcile bank statement with check register (schedule 45 minutes).

- Second Week: Pay bills, file paid bills and update check register (schedule 30 to 60 minutes).

- Third Week: Record previous months' actual deposits and expenses onto a simple worksheet, and compare actual figures with projected figures. Celebrate your victories and be curious about discrepancies (schedule 30 to 60 minutes).

- Fourth Week: Pay bills, file paid bills and update check register (schedule 30 to 60 minutes).

Step 4. An adequate paper flow system is essential to your cash flow system. Set up a system to fit your workspace. Basically, you need to break paper flow into two categories: current bills/statements for desk top, and document storage for files

Wherever clutter appears will quickly show you which areas need to be addressed. If this is not your talent in life, ask a friend to help you or hire a professional organizer! Many wishes for your true prosperity.

MORE TIPS

✦ Determine how frequently you'd like to pay bills each month, and then divide a worksheet into that number of sections. List bills in each section by due date, then determine how far ahead those bills need to be mailed to be on time. Next (the most important step), write those dates in your appointment book for the remainder of the year. Now, if you add up your income and discover that it exceeds the amounts of your monthly bills (including the prorated amount you would pay monthly for bills you actually pay quarterly, semi-annually or annually), you'll have a balanced budget, too!

✦ Have as many of your monthly bills as you can converted to automatic payment by your bank. Then all you have to do is log the payments into your checkbook. This saves time when you pay bills because it eliminates check-writing, as well as addressing and stamping envelopes. It will also save you in postage costs and more frequent trips to the post office for supplies.

4

CHANGE

"Change everything, except your loves."

— Voltaire

THE DILEMMA OF CHANGE
Priscilla Carvalho

The idea of change evokes different ideas and emotions among people. To some individuals, change may be a welcome breath of fresh air; to others it is a disruptive nuisance. Despite the inevitable stress that accompanies change, change itself deserves an honest and objective look.

For example, it can be delightful when someone, such as a professional organizer, steps forward to offer a fresh perspective on how to improve efficiency or simplify repetitive tasks. Asking "Why do we do it this way?" can be a powerful inquiry which will eventually cut through the status quo to reveal a better way.

The dilemma of change is that during the course of change, things may deteriorate before they improve. The stress of implementing a new system coupled with the pressures of daily routine can lead to a certain level of frustration that, in turn, may result in regression to old methods. In fact, it is inevitable that any system in the process of change will deteriorate before it improves.

37

Working with a professional organizer in the process of change will tend to minimize false expectations one may have and reduce being confronted with unpleasant surprises. It is fantasy to believe that instant and positive results can be achieved. It is very important to plan a realistic timetable for implementing change. Good change management will make one's progress smooth through the transitional phase until the time when the fruits of change become tangible.

The result of perseverance in the use of a new system will pay off in increased self-confidence and, consequently, improved efficiency and ease. Careful positioning of the new process is imperative. The challenge for both the professional organizer and the client is to persevere with diligence and optimism, while becoming more comfortable with the new system.

Remember, change is a powerful ally. By persevering during the transitional phase, a brilliant future is inevitable!

5

CHILDREN

"Life affords no greater responsibility, no greater privilege, than the raising of the next generation."

— C. Everett Koop, M.D.

STAYING ORGANIZED WITH CHILDREN; KEEPING CHILDREN ORGANIZED
Beth Blair

Holidays

At the beginning of the holiday season, sit down with your family and decide which events and traditions you want to participate in. Using a calendar with large square spaces, write, draw, or use a sticker to show when activities are scheduled. For example, use a house shape to indicate a trip to Grandma's, a tree for the day you will select a Christmas tree, a dreidel for the first day of Hanukkah, cookies on a day you plan to bake, a car or plane on a travel day. Children gain a great sense of security by knowing what will happen in advance. This method also allows you to pace holiday activities and commitments.

Ask the children to select some of their toys to be donated to children who have little or none. It reminds them about the spirit of giving, and provides some much needed space when they will be receiving new things.

When all those mail order catalogs begin arriving before the holidays, let the kids cut out pictures and make a "wish book."

Travel

When traveling by car, use a 13" X 9" cake pan with a plastic cover as a lap desk for each child. It can hold a lot of play things and provides a hard surface for games and drawing.

A surprise bag with new items can be used as incentive for children's cooperation while getting under way, and the novelty of something new and different can absorb a child's attention during the trip.

Buy an inexpensive or one-time-use camera for each child. Kids love having their own memories of the trip and a child as young as five or six is generally capable of operating the camera.

For air travel, give each child his own backpack. Children can then carry on crayons, cards, small games, an extra sweatshirt, a "lovey" toy or blanket. Even small toddlers can usually manage this. (If energy flags, you can easily sling one of the straps over your arm!)

Carry dehydrated baby food when traveling by plane. Hot water and paper cups are usually available for easy mixing at meal time.

Ask about airline bassinets when traveling with an infant on a jet. They hang on the wall of the bulkhead and are great for sleeping baby (built-in vibrations!). "Self-contained" toys without small pieces are ideal for travel. Some examples are Etch-a-Sketch, Magna-Doodle, tape player with head phones, Travel Yahtzee.

Barbie

Many parents have asked how to deal with the many tiny items that Barbie lovers seem to collect. Here are some ideas (these are transferable to many tiny, multi-piece toys):

Use an old luggage cosmetic case (can sometimes be found at garage sales).

Assign one drawer for Barbie dolls, clothes and accessories. At clean-up time everything can be dumped into the drawer. For young children, tape a picture to the front of the drawer, or paint each drawer a different color. Then remind them that "Barbie things go into the red drawer." They'll catch on quickly!

A divided office supply tray or food container provides lots of little sections so you can categorize tiny items such as shoes and dishware.

A small child's suitcase or tote bag allows for ready transportation on visits, car trips, doctor visits and other outings.

Toys

Put a simple code on the back of each piece to a puzzle. For young children, use colored dots or shapes. For older kids you can use numbers or letters. This saves lots of time when the pieces get mixed.

Use a plastic cleaning caddy to hold a group of play items like crayons, synthetic "dough," audio tapes, painting supplies, etc.

Use a rolling cart or stacking bins next to a toddler's kitchen set to hold all the pretend food and play dishes that tend to accumulate there.

Keep messy supplies up high so that you, the parent, decides when it's time to use finger paint and permanent markers.

Ask someone who works in an office to bring home white paper from the recycling bins for coloring and painting.

The butcher counter at a supermarket may be willing to sell a roll of wide white paper for use in projects.

Babies

Use a rolling cart as a "command center" when you are breastfeeding to keep burping cloths, bra pads, baby socks, blankets, etc. in one convenient place. Everything will be close at hand when your are unable to get up and down easily.

Create a diapering station where you need it—in the family room, laundry room or on the second floor—not just in the baby's room. A woven basket can hold basic supplies attractively and be moved easily for restocking.

A plastic cleaning caddy can hold all bottle supplies on the counter or in a cabinet.

Find one style of sipper cup that you like, then buy three to one dozen all the *same*. This makes it much easier to match lids to cups.

Plastic bibs can be run through the washing machine for thorough and easy cleaning. Hang them on the line to dry to extend the life of the bib.

If you are saving clothing and shoes for future use, put one size and season in each box and label the boxes accordingly. Sample box labels are: Size 7 shoes, Size 8 shoes, 12 month summer clothes, 18 month winter clothes.

Keep a supply of empty zip-closure bags in the diaper bag. They're handy for soiled diapers, clothing and bibs, as well as leaky bottles and other unexpected crises.

When you cook for the family, set aside portions for the baby before you add salt and spices. Puree and freeze baby's portion in ice cube trays. Transfer the cubes to freezer bags when solid. Portions can be thawed and heated as needed.

Use a plastic business envelope (with a Velcro or button-and-tie closure) to transport and protect homework, books, lunch tickets, etc.

When the school lunch menu is published, ask each child to put an initial (or number) on the box for each day he wishes to purchase lunch. If you have only one child, put an "X" on the days he doesn't want the school lunch.

If you must pay cash for school lunches, get small bills and rolls of the correct coins from the bank. Fill and seal small envelopes with the amount for one lunch in each. Write each child's name and room number on the outside to prevent permanent loss if it is dropped.

NEW PARENTS: PREPARING FOR BABY

Terry Prince

Preparing for a new baby's arrival means keeping track of many small details. Here are some suggestions for making your hospital stay more pleasant and more organized *before* labor starts!

Before the Hospital

Write a list of the names and telephone numbers of all individuals you want to call from the hospital to take to the hospital with you.

Find out what the phone call billing procedure is for the hospital you plan to use.

Buy a special notebook to record all the gifts you receive. Put a check mark next to the name if you have written a thank-you note. Bring the book to the hospital to record gifts and flowers you receive while you are there.

Buy stamps for thank-you notes and birth announcements. Keep them in an envelope in your gift record notebook.

Create a small memory box for your child to hold baby's hospital ID tags, special cards, messages and baby memorabilia.

Set up an Instruction/Baby Equipment file to keep track of warranties.

Send in all product registration cards as soon as you can.

At the Hospital

Find out how to order your baby's birth certificate. In some states certificates take a month to six weeks before they can be ordered. Mark you calendar with the earliest date and order at least two copies.

Record all the gifts you receive in your notebook. Take advantage of leisure time between feedings to send thank-you notes.

After the Hospital

Apply for the baby's birth certificate.

Once you have received the birth certificate, apply for your child's social security number.

MORE TIPS

✦ Snap barrettes onto a pretty shoestring to keep them matched and visible. The strings can be put into a box or displayed on a wall.

✦ Put modeling clay and accessories in a carrying bin with handles so you can transport it to an "approved" location. This works well for all messy projects that require adult supervision.

✦ Encourage children to keep a wish list posted on the refrigerator (or someplace equally accessible and convenient) throughout the year. Each time a child says "I want this!" or "Can I have that?" simply suggest she write it on her wish list. When it comes close to a birthday or gift-giving holiday, let children review, edit and revise their lists.

✦ To sort toys use open, plastic dishpans on book shelves. You can color coordinate them by child or type of toy. This is great for such things as blocks, miniature cars, toy soldiers, doll clothes, etc.

✦ Use clear plastic storage boxes to store children's toys with many small pieces. If the toy could be confused with other toy sets, attach a picture (depicting as fully as possible the parts of that toy) to the lid of the box. Sources for this picture include the box itself and advertising brochures found in the boxes. This enables children and their caretakers to put away toys properly.

✦ On a regular basis ask your children to decide which toys they are willing to pass along. Donate these to a pre-school, doctor's office or women's shelter, or swap with another family. (This is especially helpful right before holidays and birthdays!)

✦ In each child's closet keep a cardboard box with a lid to collect outgrown clothes. Clear it out three or four times a year (or label with the contents' size and season, if you wish to save them.)

✦ Use open-front stack bins inside a closet for easy access. They allow you and your child to sort, put away, or choose clothing quickly.

✦ If you have several children and clothes are handed down from one to another, use a permanent making pen to mark the oldest child's clothing with an X. Mark the next oldest with two Xs, and so on. As each article of clothing is passed down, just add one more X. Each child can identify his own clothes and it makes sorting clean laundry much easier.

✦ Purchase a sturdy plastic trash container with a lid for each child's room to serve as a hamper for dirty clothes. It not only contains the clothes and their odor, it makes it as easy for youngsters to put their clothing into the basket as to drop it on the floor and will help them learn to take responsibility for getting their dirty clothes into the laundry.

✦ To avoid putting multiple holes in the walls, here are two suggestions:

Put two finishing nails in the child's room wall. You can just push new paintings and drawings onto the nails and hang them right over yesterday's picture. As the nails become full, remove some of the older ones from the back to make room for new ones. The kids are proud to have lots of art work up on their walls.

Purchase an appropriate size of school bulletin board material at the lumber yard to hang in your child's room. Cover it with a light colored fabric (twin bed sheets are great for this purpose). Children can use push pins to hang up posters, banners, drawings, etc. and change them whenever they want. It's fun to see how interests changed over the years .

✦ Because it is nearly impossible to save every piece of artwork a child creates, consider recycling it in the form of a card to grandparents, or use it to wrap a gift the next time your child is invited to a birthday party.

✦ Give your children special days of the week. The child whose day it is gets to do everything that day (sit in the front seat of the car, get the mail, choose TV programs, as well as chores such as taking out the trash and clearing the table). As the children grow, so do their special day privileges and responsibilities. The trick here is to balance the privileges and chores.

✦ For teenagers who share a small bathroom with limited counter and storage space, provide each with an attractive basket. Make sure it has a good handle and is large enough to hold cosmetics, hair preparations and personal toiletries. The baskets, which are kept in their rooms, not only keep the bathroom uncluttered, they keep grooming supplies organized as well.

✦ Let children have their own color-coded cards for friends' numbers in your main family rolling card file.

✦ Keep a decorative tin by the kitchen telephone to hold scissors, ruler, pencils and pens, transparent and masking tape, string, sticky notes and plain paper. From a young age give each child its own set of these supplies and teach them that the supplies by the kitchen phone are for everyone's use and need to stay by the phone.

✦ Captain's beds are a great solution to the storage needs of small bedrooms.

✦ When a child has a friend stay overnight, a piece of thick foam rubber makes a handy extra bed. In between sleep-overs, the foam can be rolled up and stored on the closet shelf.

From the Lillian Vernon Catalog

6
CLOSETS

"Put your closet in order and the state of your mind will follow."

— Connie Cox & Chris Evatt
from *Simply Organized*

CLOSET TUNE-UP
Kathleen Poer

Today we have many material objects and limited space in which to store them. We have to be cognizant of options available to us so that we can make the best possible use of our spaces. No longer can one small closet with a single pole handle our wardrobe. We need to be objective and open to new ideas and ways to store our belongings.

The easiest place to start is to size up your closet. To do this first rearrange your wardrobe by type of garment (blouses together, skirts together, etc.). Next sort items within categories by color. Finally, arrange garment categories in descending order of length: i.e., long gowns, robes and jumpsuits first, followed by dresses, trousers, blouses and jackets in order. Now you can begin to see just how much space that is available in your closet area.

After you have done this first exercise, then rearrange the items that you have in your dresser drawers. These should be

51

organized so that items that get the most use are in drawers at the heights that make sense for your ease of access.

Next it's time to analyze just what you have in your wardrobe. What is taking up space in your closet? Consider each item and determine if it is still in good condition, stylish, and works with other items in your wardrobe. If you haven't worn it in some time, why not? Does it belong in your closet? If you have a hard time with this process, ask a friend to help you be objective and weed out the items that no longer suit you. Designate a place to store those items that you're not quite ready to let go of, and review them in six months or at the start of the next season. If after that time they still haven't been worn, it's time to re-cycle.

Good clothes can be taken to a second-hand store on consignment. Items also can be donated to a local nonprofit organization, sold at garage sales, or given to the Red Cross for international relief. We should always think in terms of recycling. If clothes are reviewed twice annually it's easy to keep on top of those that need to be recycled. They will be in better condition and of better value to whomever receives them.

If a garment doesn't fit, the color isn't right, and/or you have nothing to wear with it, it needs to go. How much you paid for it doesn't matter, it has no value to you now, but it may have great value to someone else.

Once you have pared down, it is time to take inventory of what you *do* have and wear. How much of your wardrobe is out of season? If you have a small closet in your bedroom, you should thing about storing your out of season wardrobe in another location of your house.

Before you determine where your wardrobe is best stored, take a trip through your house to find all of the places that you can find to store items. Measure all of the closets in your home, evaluate what you are storing in each and how often you use those items.

Do you have a linen closet? Is it too deep to store your linens conveniently? It's best to keep linens stored where they are used: the sheets for each bedroom in the bedroom and towels in the bathroom, if possible, or in the closest bedroom. Then it's possible to turn a linen closet into a hanging closet, if that is what you need. A 24-inch wide linen closet, transformed, will hold 48 inches of short garments hanging in two rows stacked on top of each other. You can also use the back of the door for extra storage: racks for small items, shoes, hooks, or belt and tie racks.

Is there an awkward closet under the stairs? With some rearranging can you get more usable space out of it? Is there an attic, basement or garage that can house a closet? Can you change the use of an armoire, chest, trunk, window seat or cabinet to better solve your storage needs? We have stored office supplies in an armoire, sewing projects in a trunk, and stereo systems in cabinets. There are many options for you to consider.

Get started soon to tune up your closets. A good storage tune-up will save you time and money. Not only will you know exactly what you have, you will locate everything much more quickly.

MORE TIPS

✦ Store sweaters, purses, scarves. belts and other accessories stacked in clear plastic shoe boxes. They are much easier to see.

✦ Use plastic shower curtain rings on vinyl-coated-type closet organizers for hanging and organizing scarves and belts, etc. This keeps them within easy reach and wrinkle-free!

✦ If you own more than three pairs of shoes, get them off the floor of the closet.

✦ Let shoes air out overnight before putting them back into the closet.

✦ Cycle out-of-season clothes to another room or closet, or into idle luggage stored under the bed.

✦ Consider replacing all your wire hangers with one design and color. A closet will be more orderly if all hangers are uniform. Use plastic tubular, wooden or padded hangers to hold clothes securely. Buy sturdy hangers. Plastic tubular hangers can be purchased by the dozen at larger drug and variety stores. Commercial fixture catalogs show heavy-duty hangers at volume prices. Recycle wire hangers by returning them to your favorite dry cleaner. If you must use wire hangers, keep extras in a box that allows them to be stored upright when not in use. This will prevent a lot of tangles and tempers!

✦ Closet organizing systems will increase usable space and improve visibility in almost any closet that has the traditional shelf and pole. You do-it-yourselfers can get good results with a modular, self-installed system; or you can hire a closet company to design and install one for you.

✦ If you haven't worn it in the last two years and don't love it, either recycle it or toss it; or store it for six months and *then* toss it.

✦ Keep a basket of clothing "maintenance" supplies in your closet. Include small scissors (for clipping threads), sweater shaver, lint brush, safety pins, earring backs, masking tape (to remove lint), threaded needles (1 white thread, 1 black thread), clear nail polish (for runs in nylons), steamer or travel iron, and shoe polish kit.

7
CLUTTER

"Have nothing in your house that you do not know to be useful or believe to be beautiful."

— Henry David Thoreau

CONQUERING CLUTTER
Joan Craig

Keep a box or basket in each room to receive items that don't belong in that room, but which you don't want to walk around distributing constantly. To straighten up a room you simply put all the "foreign" items in a box or basket in that room. When you are done straightening one room, the basket is then ready for redistributing things to other rooms of the home. This can be done in two ways, as follows:

If, because of time constrictions, you want to distribute the contents of only one room's container, you can walk only that box around from room to room.

If you want to return everything to its rightful room, you can bring all the boxes to a central point such as the kitchen table, and re-sort the contents destined for each room into their appropriate containers.

The Benefits of This System

- This is an excellent way to teach children a system for keeping things in order. Many people are overwhelmed later in life because they have never been taught such a system.

- When as many people as possible are involved, family members experience a valuable sense of cooperation. Sorting out containers also provides a setting for families to share with each other the events of their day while they work on a cooperative venture.

- It provides a way to make keeping the house in order a pleasant experience, because family members are gathered around a table doing something they enjoy and not forced to "clean up your room" alone.

- It teaches children that they also have a responsibility to maintain the family quarters and that it should not all be left up to an already overworked parent.

- It limits the area where lost items can be found. If someone is missing something, once the family is in the habit of putting everything that doesn't belong in a room in the basket, all anyone has to do to find a lost item is to go from room to room looking in each basket.

Like any other system, this one takes time to get used to and time to make into a habit. But the rewards are worth the effort: better family interaction, shared labor, less time wasted looking for lost items and a more orderly home.

MORE TIPS

✦ Holding onto clutter keeps you stuck in the past, frustrated with the present, and blocked from achieving your most precious dreams in the future. Yet it is often difficult to let go of accumulated possessions. The following are some affirmations you can use to reinforce the habit of letting go of things that no longer serve you. Use these also to invent some affirmations of your own to help you lighten your load.

Affirmations for Pack Rats

- I am enough.
- I have enough.
- I let go of excess baggage easily.
- I only bring a new possession into my life when I have created a vacuum to receive it.
- I surround myself only with things that are beautiful or useful to me now.
- I am gentle with myself, and not judgmental.
- I maintain a sense of humor about my excess of attachments.

✦ When the accumulation overwhelms you, pick one small area to organize, set a time limit for working, turn on the answering machine and do as much as you can in the time allotted. Be sure to include preparation and cleanup time in your plan. Then schedule another session and do the next part. This works best if you make it a rule to respect the space you've cleared out.

✦ Instead of thinking of all the stuff you need to get rid of, start from the "zero-based budgeting" position; for example, decide that you need, say, ten dishes and four saucepans. Select what you need from what you have and *get rid of the rest.*

✦ Don't let a notion about scarcity weigh you down. The universe will provide what you need when you need it. Get rid of excess. Don't keep something just because you think you "might need it some day." If you can't think of why you need it now, the chances are very small that you will need it later. If it turns out that you do want the item or something similar at some point in the future, you will also have the opportunity and resources to acquire it then.

✦ Was your mother's favorite expression "A place for everything, and everything in its place?" She was right: you can't put something away if you don't have a place to put it.

✦ Many useful objects aren't used because they are stored away from the place where they are needed. Either store them where they can be reached or get rid of them.

✦ To help you decide whether an item is worth keeping ask yourself some questions such as: "When did I use this last?" "What would I use it for?" "What do I have that I use instead of this?" "Would it make any difference to me if I didn't have it?"

✦ Place waste baskets strategically and empty them regularly. Inadequate, overflowing wastebaskets contribute to household clutter. How can you throw it away if there's no place to throw it?

✦ Start the process of sorting your clutter by grouping it into broad categories:

- Definitely trash. (Get it into the bin.)
- Give it away. (Box it up and deliver it to your favorite charity.)
- Keep it and use it. (Find a place for it and put it there.)
- Needs repair. (Take it to your car, or put it where "gizmos-I-have-to-fix" live.)

- I don't know if I really want it/need it/can use it. Pack in a clearly labeled box, and in six months, if you have not looked into it, give the box away without opening it.)

✦ If living with a clutter collector is driving you crazy, please remember that you can't change his style. Your best bet is to get him to agree to contain his things in a specific area and get his cooperative permission to keep his stuff out of the common areas. You may still have to pick up after him, but at least he won't be angry when you pile another load of stuff on his bed. Remember, the operative phrase is "cooperative permission." Assign responsibility where it belongs.

✦ One person's "junk" may be another person's treasure. Get in the habit of identifying your junk and recycling it so someone who will love it can find it. Pass on those expensive gee-gaws and useless gifts from well-meaning friends. Dispose of broken gadgets beyond repair. Make room for things you need, love, and can use.

8

COMPUTERS

"To err is human, but to really foul things up requires a computer."

— Anonymous

TO COMPUTERIZE OR NOT TO COMPUTERIZE
Leslie K. Martin

A computer is both a major purchase and a major time commitment. The decision to buy should not be made based on what is fashionable. Today the average small business will spend anywhere between $3,000 and $7,500 on computer equipment. For $7,500 the average office could completely redo its filing system, replace a couple of desks, buy a copy machine, get new phone equipment—and even slap on a fresh coat of paint.

Purchasing the system is only the front-end financial burden. Once you have the computer sitting in your office, you'll spend an average of six months (more if this is your first contact with one) learning how to utilize it efficiently, setting up systems that work for your business, and keying data into the programs. Allow even more time and money for each employee who must learn to use it.

Why, then, would anyone ever start down this trail of sure-fire madness and poverty? Because owning a computer is like having a personal assistant, time manager, bookkeeper, in-house publishing company and one-person marketing agency all in one. Because a computer will expand your capabilities and allow you to be more creative than you ever dreamed. Because a computer will challenge you like a good chess game can. Because once you make peace with this infuriating, droning, glowing, mechanical being (and it *will* assume a personality all its own) you will produce quality and quantity far beyond what any one person has a right to do (and be able to charge for it). But most of all, because of the feeling you'll get whenever you look at the masterpieces you're going to create.

Major Factors in the Decision to Buy

Do you know what a computer can do for you? As a computer consultant I am continually amazed by clients who wave money in my face and say "Let's go shopping!", when they haven't a clue what the basic application areas are and don't understand how these could be practically applied to their businesses. Do you know the definition of (and difference between) a word processor and a page-layout program, or a database and a spreadsheet? You could conceivably accomplish the same tasks on an accounting, data base or spreadsheet program, but they have distinct differences, and each excels in specific areas.

Do you already have administrative systems established in your business? Many people consider a computer a panacea for chaos and lack of know-how. If your current systems are a mess, the computer can quickly double that mess for you. Computers can produce paper faster than you can dispose of it. If you don't have a definite plan of attack, or chose a few specific problems you have to solve, a computer won't be of much help. A computer does *not* supply you with knowledge or common sense. If you don't understand double-entry bookkeeping in your paper ledger, you'll be lost with a computer accounting package. Don't expect it to teach you accounting principles (although it *can* fool you into believing it's teaching you how to play the piano).

A computer *does* give you a multitude of tools to use. It is up to you to learn what to do with them.

Have you had any hands-on experience in using a computer? An IBM PC or compatible and an Apple Macintosh® are two distinctly different entities. You will have very different experiences with each. Your computer is a machine you will be living with every working day for the next few years. For the money you will be paying and the time commitment involved, make sure you *do not* plug anything into your office outlet that you haven't taken for a test drive. Try out various keyboards *and* the programs you want to purchase. Test them alone, without the "helpful" assistance of sales staff hanging over your shoulder, showing you with lightening moves how "easy" it all is. Take samples of your real work with you, and use a machine that will be hooked up with the equipment, applications and cables you will be buying. How long should a hands-on preliminary test on a potential purchase be? Long enough for you to reach the stage where you can say, "Okay, I can make this thing do what I need it to."

Do you like computers? What I'm asking goes beyond surface intimidation. Will you get angry every time you look at this noisy, plastic box in your roomful of antique wood furnishings? Do you find you just don't seem to "think" computer, and the way programs operate seems totally foreign to you? When something goes wrong, do you panic and shut the stupid thing off, or tough it out until you analyze what's happening? There are some people who simply don't find computers a natural fit. A custom program, intensive training, a personal tutor or simply turning the machine over to others on your staff who are "computer simpatico" might be potential solutions.

Are you ready to do this? If you aren't ready for it, if you can't find the time to learn how to use it, don't buy it. If you buy it, commit time to it each week (each day is best, so that what you learned last week isn't forgotten before you use it again).

Decide what you want the computer to do for you, learn what programs will best suit your specific needs and business situation, use the computer you want to purchase, determine if you "think" computerese, and then make the commitment to put in the time to learn about it—and your computer will become a wonderful, dependable, invaluable production tool that will give you and your business many happy hours of quality product and service.

COMPUTER CARE & MAINTENANCE
Leslie K. Martin

Back up, back up, back up!!! Always make copies of your files. There are two kinds of computer operators: those who have had a hard drive crash on them, and those who will. A hard drive is a mechanical object. Mechanical objects eventually *fail*. If the document you are working on is worth the time it took for you to build it in the first place, then it's definitely worth the few minutes it takes to back it up.

Buy a surge protector. Electricity is a varying commodity. It does not always supply an even amount of power: in fact, it surges. If you get an unexpected burst of electricity your computer can, almost literally, be fried. Surge protectors help by shutting the power off when an unexpected jolt occurs.

Do not lay diskettes next to anything that contains a magnet or the diskette might be erased. Anything that plugs in can generate electromagnetic fields that might cause damage— your copier, phone, or answering machine, and even parts of your computer.

Keep the computer and diskettes away from direct sunlight and avoid exposure to moisture.

During a thunder or electrical storm, if there is any danger of the power going out, turn the computer off. If static electricity is high, ground yourself, by touching something else first, before you use the computer. Even a small amount of static can short out the machine.

If the electricity ever does go out while the computer is running, immediately turn the equipment off, and wait until it's safe. You will likely lose whatever file was open unless you had just finished saving it. It is always wise to save your work every fifteen minutes or so.

It is very hard on the machinery to stop and start the computer. It is better to leave the computer on than to turn it off for an hour and then back on, but don't let it run unattended for many hours at a time.

Clean the monitor screen only with a soft cloth. The protective chemical filter on the screen can easily be scratched by paper or cleaning solutions.

The rolling ball on the bottom of the mouse picks up lint and paper scraps from the mouse pad, and the ball will eventually jam. For this reason, keep the mouse pad clean. Clean the ball itself by quickly dunking it in rubbing alcohol. Consult your user manual for instructions on removing the ball from the mouse.

Jammed wires and heat can cause the computer to malfunction. Make sure there is clearance between the wires at the back of the machine and any wall or furniture.

Dust kills. Cover your keyboard and printer when not in use. Buy a tiny vacuum at a computer store and keep your keyboard and the surface of your computer dust free.

When using a portable computer in a plane, check the air carrier's regulations first. Carry it in a well-padded shoulder bag. At your hotel, check the voltage before you plug it in for a recharge.

Buy a utility program that will un-erase accidentally erased files and fix damaged ones. This may someday save you major aggravation.

MORE TIPS

✦ Computer printers eat electricity (my Macintosh® laser printer runs on 700 watts), and can make the lights in your home flicker. Turn the printer off when not in use for long periods (a long "printer period" is shorter than a long "monitor period").

✦ Use your computer to print file labels. You can establish a format and all labels will be consistent and easy to read.

✦ On PC computer files, use 3-dot extensions to categorize clients or subjects, for example, ARL-STRY.NAP for Arleen's story for the NAPO newsletter.

✦ Use your word processor to keep both a personal journal and a professional journal or to explore and express thoughts, ideas and/or feelings on any subject that has your attention. It is a marvelous way to access and record any number of emotions and creative ideas. Use it to brainstorm, to sort things out, to help you to better understand a problem, project or goal. Record your likes, dislikes, the pros and cons. Let your fingers fly and see what appears on the screen.

✦ **Back up! Back up! Back up!** (Worth repeating.) For valuable (hard to reconstruct) information, a copy should be stored at another home or office weekly or monthly. In case of theft or fire, it won't take too long to re-enter the missing information. Also, for files with a great number of entries, you can make a backup disk for, say, each day of the week (five or seven backup disks) and label them accordingly. Don't store them right by the computer in case of theft.

✦ Make paper copies of documents only when you must. Backup disks save paper.

✦ Keep a dictionary, a wordfinder and computer software manuals right by the computer.

✦ Treat your computer desktop as you would your filing cabinet. Use folders with appropriate subject headings to file individual documents or programs.

✦ Periodically do as you do in your home: Empty the wastebaskets and take out the trash.

68

9

CONTAINERS

"What wonderful containers a container can contain."

— Theodore Roethke.

There are all sorts of boxes, bags, bins, shelves, drawer dividers and desk trays available. Even though a particular kind of container was made for a specific use, you may use it any way you like. Be creative!

Bags

✦ For pantyhose, use a hanging shoe storage holder with clear pockets. Label each pocket with the contents, such as "black/sheer-to-waist." Be sure to dedicate one or two compartments to "damaged/wearable under pants." As necessary, refill pockets so that you will always have the required pantyhose on hand. Hang this storage holder on the inside of the closet door, or from the closet rod.

✦ Store sterling silver jewelry and non-display silver serving pieces in zipper lock storage bags or plastic wrap. Make sure you squeeze out all the air, which is the cause of tarnishing.

✦ Pint- and quart-size plastic zipper lock freezer bags (tricolor seals are highly recommended) are perfect for storing toiletries when traveling. If leakage occurs, it takes place in the plastic bag rather than on your clothes.

✦ For frequent travelers, a small travel pouch pre-packed with toiletries (which means buying double of certain items at the store) saves time when preparing for a trip.

✦ When records are retired to storage, put categories together in a large zipper lock bag with a label on the inside or outside telling the year and describing what is inside. This will make locating things much easier. For example, all credit card receipts can go in a bag with bills and ATM receipts. Bank statements are stored together with their corresponding check registers.

Baskets

✦ Rectangular plastic baskets are a boon for containing a huge variety of items. Here are some suggestions: panty hose, socks, shoulder pads, toiletries, lingerie, batteries, dog leashes, tape, pet supplies, children's socks and tights, frozen foods (place in the freezer; sort by category—vegetables, popsicles, etc.), children's underwear, office supplies, craft supplies, scrap paper, fabric (especially for quilters!), audio tapes, snacks, first aid items, toys, and large jewelry.

✦ Keep a basket on a small table next to the front door to hold all items which need to be taken out (e.g., mail, film canisters, library books, borrowed items, dry cleaning, etc.).

✦ Small wicker or plastic baskets are good for storing toiletries in the bathroom. Designate different baskets for different types of cosmetic supplies (eye makeup, blush, brushes and combs). Mugs make great containers for mascaras, eyeliners and bathroom bits and pieces. Spare toothbrushes, emery boards, lotions, toothpaste, medications and other items that clog the medicine cabinet can be stored upright to save space.

Binders

✦ To eliminate last-minute dashes to the store, use a binder with pocket pages marked with the months of the year for storing birthday, anniversary, or special holiday cards for family and friends. As you find cards throughout the year, slip them into the appropriate pages, ready for writing and mailing when that month rolls around.

Boxes

✦ Divided accordion folders neatly house your greeting card supplies. Label each section according to greeting card category.

✦ Store items you "can't bear to part with" in boxes labeled with the dates that you put them in storage. If you don't return to those items after one more year, it's time to let go of them.

✦ Shoe boxes work well for storing maps, folded flat and laid horizontally, with titles visible. Make section dividers of fairly stiff cardboard, slightly taller (longer) than the maps. Label each divider with the appropriate section name (Bay Area, North Bay counties, San Diego area, etc.)

✦ Open shoe boxes placed on shelves will make their contents easily accessible if you simply slide the one you want off the shelf, pick out what you want, and replace it. Thus, they can function almost as drawers, and may be easily retrieved even on higher, less accessible shelves.

Caution: use only sturdy boxes and strengthen them by taping the lid to the underside of its box. Decorate the boxes, if you like, with taped-on construction paper or adhesive shelf liner. Label contents with a medium or broad marker pen.

✦ Spare light bulbs store well in a shoe box, upright, with their corrugated protectors still around them.

✦ To save your eyes and eliminate repetitive searching, use boxes, stacking trays, drawers, bookshelves, cupboards or any combination of containers to sort papers into general categories that fit your needs, such as:

- **Now** (to do, call or take care of soon)

- **Shopping** (lists, ideas, errands, catalogs, order and re-order info)

- **Correspondence** (personal, business [if minimal], addresses, greeting cards, things to send to others)

- **Financial** (bills to pay, medical claims to file)

- **Filing/Soon** (paid bills, current plans/travel, important papers [taxes, insurance, investments, etc.], current business, special project activities, school papers)

- **Filing/Later** (lower priority, long-term reference)

- **House** (decorating, garden, ideas, maintenance)

- **Kitchen** (recipes, coupons, menus, entertaining, warranties, instructions [if kept in kitchen])

- **Scrapbook** (photos, memorabilia, souvenirs)

- **Reading** (magazines, newspapers, articles)

- **Throw Away** (this should be your largest container)

✦ Use clear plastic boxes for projects. Label each box with a removable label and stack the boxes with your work-in-progress projects stored inside.

10

DESKS

"Is your desk a prison where you're grueling or a garden where you're blooming?"

— Author Unknown

MANAGING YOUR DESK
Odette Pollar

How do you know whether it is time to get organized? The time is now if, upon scanning the piles on your desk, you have said, "I can lay my hands on anything" and then couldn't. If the bulk of your day seems to be filled with shuffling papers, and those papers actually hinder your getting other, more important, work done; or if you are overwhelmed and mystified about where to put all those memos, reports, drafts, bills, magazines, correspondence, miscellaneous documents and mail that comes to you, it's time to change.

Think of your entire desk as *prime space*. Anything that stays this close to you must earn its keep. When sorting, the guiding principle is to put *like* things together. Starting with the drawers, sort these by consolidating, dumping and rearranging. Throw away the unused, dried up, old or unidentifiable items. Limit your personal items to part of one drawer.

73

Consider placing the stapler and scotch tape in a desk drawer. The phone, business card holder, desk calendar, stapler, electric pencil sharpener, tape dispenser, holder for paper clips, calculator, radio, a cup containing miscellaneous pens and pencils, and framed photos, do not all need to live in the open, crowding your workspace.

The top of the desk should support only the most critical items. You must process everything on your desk by putting it into its proper location quickly and easily. Ask yourself these questions when you pick up a piece of paper:

- To what does the item refer?
- To what category should it belong?
- What is the next step I must take?

To begin sorting, start with one stack of papers at a time. Sort from the top down. Do not move one or two items to see what interesting things reside below. No matter how overwhelming it may seem, all of these loose papers will sort themselves out into logical groupings. Some materials will naturally go with related documents. A surprising amount will be thrown away because they are no longer relevant or have already been handled. Some will represent projects where the next step belongs to someone else. Be sure to send it along with a note. One or two items will be things you had just been looking for the other day and they need to be dealt with immediately.

What to do about all of the little pieces of paper? Throw some away, of course. Record all appointments on your calendar. Integrate into your To Do list those tasks that can be accomplished in the next couple of days. In the future, write notes in the appropriate place initially—for instance: on the inside cover of the file folder; on the bottom of client correspondence or on an internal memo form.

Skim items to be read and decide on their importance. If you will take the time to read something, then file it immediately according to the subject to which it refers. Once you make a decision on any piece of paper, process or file it promptly. Once you get organized, maintain your system by establishing good paper management habits. Be very select about what you keep and throw away. Recycle as much as possible. Resist the tendency to set it aside *just for a minute.*

To ensure that piles do not multiply, spend 15 minutes at the end of each day clearing off the top of your desk. Put away your active files so your desk is clean in the morning. This is the best way to stay ahead. One day's accumulation is easily handled. Always re-file things quickly. Keep your organizing system and your files simple, easy and logical. You will be able to get and stay organized by breaking the habits that lead to clutter. You deserve a clean, clear workspace.

EIGHT TIPS FOR NATIONAL CLEAN OFF YOUR DESK DAY
Karen Rossum

1. Pick a time you know you can do it. Mark your calendar. Be realistic about how long it will take.

Suggestion for supervisors: Set aside an hour or two for your entire staff to get organized. You won't be interrupted, and everyone can share the feelings of accomplishment.

2. Have supplies on hand before you begin. Consider trash bags, file folders, hanging files, labels, storage boxes, marking pens, rubber bands, dust rags and cleaning products.

3. Arrange equipment, supplies and files in your workspace according to the *frequency of use* principle. (See box next page.)

USE	LOCATION
Daily	On top of primary work area
Weekly	Inside desk
Monthly	In same room
Less than monthly	In another room

4. Sort all loose papers and folders into: Trash/Recycle, For Storage, To be Filed, For Others, To Do.

Be sure to send along a note with papers referred to others. Prioritize each piece as you put it into the To Do pile. If your To Do stack is more than one inch thick, schedule time to prioritize. Be decisive. Complete each paper before going on to the next.

5. Use an In box. Label it with your name and the words "In Box." Put it in a location that's obvious and convenient for everyone. An empty In box encourages others to use it. A consistently full In box invites co-workers to put materials on their place of choice—your chair, telephone, computer, or wherever they think it will get your attention.

6. Use a calendar or day-planner. Review it frequently. Allow for meeting preparation and travel time between appointments. Schedule appointments with yourself to work on projects and answer phone calls. Schedule follow-up appointments at the end of your meeting. When you expect a co-worker to return something to you, mark the day on your calendar.

7. Sort unwanted mail into a waste basket or recycling bin. Throw away junk immediately. If you are pressed for time, open only First Class mail. If you are someone's assistant, get permission to do this for them.

8. Clear your desk off daily. Sitting down to a clean desk invites clarity, creativity and choice. It is a sign that you are in control of your workload and your environment.

THE ART OF DESK MANAGEMENT
Scott Plakun

Cluttered desks are a chronic problem in office environments. If you've convinced yourself that your cluttered desk contributes to your creativity, think again. A cluttered desk conveys a negative impression to many people, including:

Your customers. You can't do a good job of customer support if you can't find the information you need to answer questions. And with a cluttered desk, you're more likely to misplace that phone message from the client who wants to hear from you.

Your manager. A cluttered desk tells your manager that you are functioning near capacity. That can cause you to be passed over for promotions—even if your boss' desk is more cluttered than yours. Who said life was fair?

If your whole work area is in need of attention, you may want to hire a professional organizer. If it's just your desk that needs help, these few simple steps will work:

1. Prepare. Create a simple A-Z file in the desk drawer closest to you. Have your personal planner close at hand.

2. Stack. Put all of the papers on your desk in one stack. Don't pay attention to the size, shape, color or content.

3. Process. This may take several sittings, depending on the size of your stack. Pick up the top item in the stack and make one of these choices:

- **Do it.** If you can complete the item quickly, do it.

- **Delegate it.** If it should be delegated, make a note in your planner to remind you when to delegate it and to whom. Put the item in your A-Z file.

- **Decide to do it later.** Make the appropriate notation in your planner and put the item in your A-Z file.

- **Discard it.** If you don't need it, throw it away or recycle it. Now.

4. Keep at it. Use the same process for each new item as it arrives. If clutter starts to develop, use the same process to eliminate it.

An uncluttered desk helps you get more done. When you have a stray thought it only takes a moment to locate the item and make a note of your thought before returning to your selected task. Try it; you'll like it!

MORE TIPS

✦ If you don't have a desk or adequate drawer space, keep your jar of pens, paper clip holder, stapler, and other tools on a tray. A tray provides a defined place to keep things in an orderly fashion. Then, if the space is needed for work, you can simply move the tray and replace it when you're finished.

✦ Put things you use most often in the areas of your desk you can reach without moving, such as the front of the top side drawers. Since you have to move to get to them, the middle and bottom drawers are the places for things you don't use as often but want close at hand. The backs of all drawers and the far corners of the desktop are the place for things you use the least.

✦ Remember: Desks are not storage areas; they are work surfaces. Well-used desk space contains materials that enable you to be productive within arm's reach (scissors, paper clips, your datebook, stamps). Things that don't need to be within arm's reach belong in a storage cabinet or drawer (a year's supply of business cards, last year's Christmas cards that you intend to answer, the postage scale you use once a month, the other nine boxes of staples that came in the carton) .

Also, efficient use of space and materials dictates, with most supplies, that you keep close by only one of whatever you use regularly: *one* pair of scissors, *one* bottle of white correction fluid, *one* staple remover, *one* letter opener, *one* stapler and *one* box of staples. Store extra supplies in a closet or cabinet away from your work surface. (In addition to space considerations, unopened supplies have a longer shelf life than opened ones.)

✦ Save time (and your back) by following this general principle: Use shelves located between waist and eyes for things you use most often. Use shelves between your waist and the floor for items you use less often. Least used items belong on the shelves over your head. If you live in a location prone to earthquakes, be sure highest shelves are equipped with some kind of restraint that will keep books and other items stored on them from falling on your head during a tremor.

✦ If your desk is a mess, create the illusion of order quickly by stacking everything in one *neat* pile to clear some space. Then sort from the top down, one piece at a time (don't skip around) into four or five main categories: Finances, To Do, To Read, To File and To Delegate. These broadly-sorted categories can be subdivided later into narrower categories to assist in scheduling your time to complete the actions required.

✦ Open, sort and file mail as soon as you can. If you absolutely cannot get to it right away, set up a simple desktop system of folders or bins to make a place for mail to be sorted each day (see previous tip). Put the system in a place where the unsorted mail is collecting now. Don't forget to use the trash can!

✦ Tidy your desk every night, and get it ready for the next morning.

11

EARTHQUAKE
PREPAREDNESS

"Any disaster you can survive is an improvement in your character, your stature and your life. What a privilege!"

— Joseph Campbell

ORGANIZING YOUR VEHICLE FOR AN EARTHQUAKE OR OTHER EMERGENCY
Allison Ricks

If you live in areas prone to natural disasters, or if you are driving a long distance, it is imperative that you keep a number of essential items stored in the trunk of the car. When an earthquake or other emergency occurs, you may need to walk a long distance, you may be stuck in traffic for hours, or you may be injured and not able to travel at all.

In addition to the basic supplies to keep in your car that are listed in Chapter 1, the items below will come in handy when you're stuck away from home. Keep them neatly and safely in a trunk organizer or other suitable covered container. Check your supplies at least twice yearly. Note the expiration date on perishable items. Always replace outdated items and items you use up right away.

- Aerosol can flat tire inflator
- Collapsible camping shovel
- Extra clothing, such as a sweat suit, jacket, jeans, shirt, and sweater. If you must walk, you may be more comfortable in this type of clothing, and you may need extra clothing for warmth.
- Newspaper (to spread or lie on or kneel on)
- Plastic trash bags
- Fire extinguisher
- Rope
- Sealed bottled water (at least one gallon per person). Change the water at least twice per year. April and October, when we change between standard time to daylight time, are good times to do this.
- Short rubber hose for siphoning gas or water
- Small tool kit
- Windshield ice scraper

If in an emergency you must leave your car, put a note on your windshield with your name, address, phone number and your destination. If you are walking, leave everything but the vital (survival) necessities in your car. You do not want to walk overloaded. *Make sure you take your money and identification with you.*

ORGANIZING YOUR OFFICE FOR AN EARTHQUAKE
Barbara Raleigh

When an earthquake occurs, the higher your location, the more motion you will feel. Swaying may cause office equipment to be thrown around. Therefore, it is vitally important that you have equipment such as computers and monitors bolted to the furniture, and furniture such as bookcases and files bolted to the walls. If you are working many stories up in a high-rise, you should also have desks bolted to the floor.

Take a serious look at your office arrangement. Do not position tall bookcases right next to desks; the books can fall out of shelves during an earthquake. Make sure files are not located where they can open and block a doorway. Even two-drawer files that open during an earthquake could stop a door from opening. Make sure that file cabinets located near desks are far enough away that the drawers cannot hit you if they open during an earthquake.

We think of emergency supplies for our homes, but *what emergency supplies do you have in your office?* When an earthquake occurs, you may need to walk home, be stranded in your office or need to travel to a shelter. To be prepared in your office, as well as in your automobile, stock a backpack or shoulder tote bag with the following itmes:

- Comfortable walking shoes and socks
- Extra clothing such as sweat suit, jacket, jeans, shirt, sweater, etc. You may be more comfortable changing if you must walk, and you may need extra clothing for warmth.
- First-aid kit
- Flashlight
- Map of local area so you can determine alternate routes home
- Mylar survival blanket or sleeping bag
- Non-perishable food. Change these when you change the water.
- Plastic trash bags
- Prescription medication taken routinely. Make sure you replace your medication before it becomes out of date.
- Sealed bottled water (at least one gallon per person). Change the bottled water at least twice per year. April

and October when we change between Standard Time and Daylight Savings Time are good times to do this.
- Toilet paper
- Waterproof matches

When earthquake occurs, keep calm, check on co-workers, and turn off all equipment. If you leave your office building, make sure you tell someone where you are going and, if possible, leave a note in your office. Use the stairs, *not an elevator*, if you leave your office building. If you are walking, leave everything but the vital (survival) necessities in your office. You do not want to walk overloaded. *Make sure you take your money and identification with you.*

12
FENG SHUI

"Cultivate peace and harmony with all."

— George Washington

FENG SHUI: ORIENTAL ART
OF HARMONIOUS PLACEMENT
Linda Lenore Graves

The Chinese art, science and philosophy known as Feng Shui has been passed down through the ages from Master to Master. Traditionally, its secrets have been shared only with the wealthy or very prestigious, and usually at great expense. It is believed among initiates that Feng Shui possesses such power that it could cause great harm and destruction if used inappropriately.

The two words in the name Feng Shui refer to wind and water, respectively—the two forces which change the shape of the earth. The principles of Feng Shui will change the shape of your life as you begin to apply them. Feng Shui can be a very spiritual experience as it reaches deeply into your being.

It is useful to think of the Art of Feng Shui as a sort of "Ecology 101," because it helps you to view and understand your environment from a new perspective. Just as "you are what you eat," as the saying goes, Feng Shui is based on the principle that you are also a product of what you see and feel in your environment. How you create and take care of the spaces where you live and work plays a major role in the shape that your life takes. Feng Shui seeks to create joy and functionality in the environment that will bring joy and usefulness into your life.

Feng Shui brings order and harmony into physical space. As each person "walks to the beat of a different drum," so each Feng Shui "solution" to improving harmony is different from environment to environment. Nevertheless, there are a few guidelines that appear to be universal. As you train yourself to become more aware of your physical space, one room at a time, you will start to recognize the beauty around you and identify the sources of discord. The more you play with applying these guidelines to fine tune your space, the greater harmony you will experience in it. This harmony will spread outward like a beautifully woven spider web or symphony to touch your family, friends, neighbors, co-workers and acquaintances.

Feng Shui has the potential to cultivate peace within each of us, and to awaken deep-seated knowledge of our connectedness to our land. To practice, you may start on a favorite room of your home. Enjoy your process!

General Information

- Build homes and rooms in square or rectangular shapes, not irregular shapes with cut outs. When designing a floor plan, avoid the projection of closets or other obstructions into a room.

- The most important area of the house should be centrally located. This could be the living room, family room, or possibly the kitchen/great room.

- The back door should not be in a direct line with the front door.

- Bring in gentle curves whenever possible.

- House doors should open inward.

- Doors that face each other should open inward and in the same direction (hinges on the same side of the frame).

- Inner and outer doors need to be exactly aligned or made obvious not to align.

- Stairs should descend at right angles to a doorway.

- Hang art work at eye level according to the function of the room: hallway artwork at eye level for walking; dining room artwork at eye level for sitting; multi-purpose room artwork should achieve a balance between levels.

- Color is an activator. Introduce into your space colors that please you or that remind you of something, for example, green for money. (Black, white, gray and beige are considered neutrals, not colors.)

- The Chinese especially do not like the number four; therefore, acquire sets of things in groups of three, if possible, or other odd numbers like five, seven or nine.

Dining Room

- The dining room should have two entrances.

- Both doors should be either on the same wall as the windows, or on walls adjacent to the windows.

- Furnishings should be minimal. Each piece should serve at least two purposes.

- Allow 20 to 26 inches of table space for each place setting.

- Allow three feet around the table for chairs to move easily in and out.

Living Room

- Use screens or plants to divide irregular shaped or L-shaped rooms into rectangular or squares.

- There should be one wall that is plain and unbroken by windows or doors.

- If there is a fireplace, it should be located on the unbroken wall.

- Seating should be square to the walls and not under overhead beams.

- Windows should have pleasant views.

Kitchen

- It is best if the kitchen is not seen from the entrance.

- Place the stove on the south side.

- Place a mirror over the back of the stove.

- There should be storage between the stove and the sink for metal pans.

- The kitchen should not be next to the bathroom.

- The stove should not be next to the bathroom.

- The kitchen and eating nook should be separated.

- The eating table should not be in the center of the kitchen.

Yard

- Do not have a large tree directly in line with the front door.

- Plant trees on the northwest side of the house to protect it.

- Have a large area to the south to bring in good fortune. A garden in this area is especially nice.

- Bring in gentle curves.

- It is good to be able to see water. Avoid having unseen water on land.

- Do not have harsh looking rocks or other formations on the land or seen from the yard.

To Celebrate Holidays

- Put appropriate items for each holiday in as many rooms as possible.

- Use candles.

- Dress up stuffed animals if possible.

- Dress up house plants with bows, decorations, lights.

- Bring in blooming plants.

- Display collections arranged in a holiday motif, e.g., in an Easter basket, in the shape of a star or tree or heart. Alternatively, decorate collections with holiday colored or designed ribbon.

NINE WAYS TO ARRANGE FOR GOOD FORTUNE IN THE NEW YEAR

Kathryn Metz

The Art of Placement is devoted to building a community of awareness of place. We invite you to join us in exploring the seen and unseen ways that place affects us—our moods, our actions, our accomplishments, our lives. In the new year, drawing upon the Chinese art of placement called Feng Shui, we can all make simple and affordable changes in our homes and workplaces that will bring clarity and peace, joy and prosperity. Here are nine ways to arrange for your good fortune in your new year.

- To help master the art of keeping your New Year's resolutions, hang a brass wind chime above your desk.

- To fulfill your wishes, see your dream come true, from beginning to end, in a sequence of nine pictures, every day for 27 days.

- To accelerate your success and prosperity, greet one new person every day for 27 days, making no requests or complaints.

- To invite opportunity to knock, fix your front door. Allow no squeaking, sticking or wobbling door knobs.

- To further your opportunities, unblock doorways and remove stored items from behind doors.

- To support your work, your vision and your commitment, sit at a desk that is spacious, allowing room for the expansion of your ideas.

- To meet this year's challenges, see in your mind's eye the faces of five people who can help you.

- To lift your spirits on a difficult day, carry with you nine round pieces of orange peel.

- And if this is your year to speak up, *sing*—in the shower, in the car, and, maybe, under the bright lights!

Good luck as you move through the new year. We celebrate your unique sense of beauty and artistry, for it enriches the power of placemaking for us all.

FENG SHUI BUSINESS TIPS
Kathryn Metz

Growing a small business requires clear direction and the mobilization of creative forces. Drawing on the Chinese art of placement called Feng Shui, owners and employees can make simple and affordable changes in the workplace that will inspire vision and purpose, engender cooperation and innovation. Here are twenty-six ways to arrange for your good business fortune.

- To call forth a clear vision, hang a brass chime just inside your office door.

- To expand the vision and awaken creativity, place a small brass bell in the middle of the right side of your desk.

- To support your vision and commitment, sit at a desk that is spacious, allowing room for the expansion of your ideas.

- For powerful decision-making, choose an office in a commanding position, such as the corner office farthest from the main door.

91

- To manage from a personal power base, place your desk facing the door with your back to a solid wall rather than a window.

- For focus and concentration, hang a chime above where you sit at your desk.

- To articulate your point of view, use red ribbon to hang a brass bell on the *inside* of your office door.

- To think creatively, place a mirror to the right and to the left of your desk.

- To deal effectively with difficult people or circumstances, sit in a high back chair.

- To enhance the company image and good name, place red flowers in the center of the wall opposite the door of your office.

- To spread the company message, hang a chime in the center of your conference room.

- To encourage team effort, light a long hallway, especially if there are many doors.

- To enlist support, envision the faces of five people who can help you.

- To implement your marketing plan, unblock doorways and remove stored items from behind doors, both at home and the office.

- To strengthen your client base, sprinkle birdseed from the main door of your office building to the sidewalk.

- For good fortune, choose a location where the previous occupants were successful.

- To improve productivity, bathroom doors should not be visible upon entering the building or office.

- To reduce stress for everyone, place two mirrors so that you walk between them as you enter the office.

- To stimulate a positive cash flow, collect a small amount of water from nine different *prosperous* financial institutions, and store it in the far left-hand corner of the office.

- To increase profits, place a mirror to draw in a view of water, a symbol of wealth.

- To boost sales, place the sales force close to the front door.

- To keep product moving, choose a retail establishment with a big back door.

- To cultivate good luck, place fresh flowers in the manager's office, the reception area and employee lounge.

- To keep business running smoothly, avoid placing desks in line with a door.

- To multiply fame and success, hang a chime over the head of your bed.

- To accelerate growth and development, greet one new person every day for 27 days, making no requests or complaints.

Good luck as you begin to develop your own unique skill in the art of placemaking. Your attention and artistry will enhance the quality of the workplace for everyone.

13

FILES

"A filing system is a place to lose things alphabetically."

— Author Unknown

CREATING A FILING SYSTEM

Anacaria Myrrha

A well-designed filing system provides reliable access to information. It is logical and consistent, and it groups information into clearly defined, unambiguous categories that reflect use. It facilitates rapid retrieval and permits new files to be integrated easily into the system.

If your filing system is used by more than one person, the development of appropriate, useful categories requires the direct involvement of *all* persons using the system. If you are the only person using the files, you can be more eccentric in your choice of names and definitions.

When deciding what to name a document file, think "retrieval." Ask yourself these questions: Under what circumstances will I need the document? Why? What will I think of when I am looking for it? Do I need to file it in two places? (If so, put in a duplicate but be careful of this one!) Do I need to put in a cross-reference? (Be willing to do so when appropriate.)

On occasion it will be necessary to make a file for a single piece of paper. Do it! Do not file your Fictitious Business Name Statement in with your business bank account information thinking you will remember where it is. You won't! Trust me on this one. More than one client who insisted on filing this way has called in a panic at ten o'clock at night asking if I remember where something is filed.

Remember, *be logical and consistent*.

Beware of using numerical systems that have no logic, or a complicated logic, behind them. They are difficult to use and maintain.

"Miscellaneous" files are the black holes of filing systems. They are places to *put* documents, not to *find* documents. Avoid them!

Systems for Classifying Information

Alphabetical by name . . . . Clients, Products
Alphabetical by subject . . . . Reference, Suppliers
Numerical . . . . Invoices, Job Numbers
Chronological . . . . Board Meetings, Scripts
Geographical . . . . Sales territories, Zip codes

---

Categories and Subject Headings

How is your filing system set up now? Do you have an A-to-Z system in which bank statements and paid bills are interspersed with the dog's inoculation records and the family genealogy? Are your taxes filed next to tender cards from your significant other?

If so, consider this alternative. Group your folders by major categories and subject headings. Think hierarchically, from the larger to the smaller. Most people's files can be divided into the three major categories of business, financial and personal files. A secondary breakdown into subjects can then be made.

For example, in an A-to-Z system, your auto insurance might be filed under *Auto, Insurance, State Farm* or the name of your agent. With the above-suggested arrangement, your auto insurance is filed in the *Financial* category and grouped with other insurance folders under the subject heading of *Insurance*.

This grouping makes filing and retrieval easy. It eliminates the number of places you might have to look for a file, and the need for duplication is obviated.

Here are some suggested subject headings under which to group folders. Add or delete according to your needs.

BUSINESS	FINANCIAL	PERSONAL
Administrative	Accountants	Auto
Associations	Banks	Books & Tapes
Clients	Banking	Correspondence
Corporate Records	Budget	Family
Correspondence	Contributions	Friends
Equipment	Credit	Household
Forms	Financial Info	Health
Legal	Financial Consult	Humor
Marketing	Financial Stmts	Memorabilia
Personnel	Insurance	Pets
Projects	Investments	Projects (by name)
Reference	Loans	Recipes
Resources	Property	Restaurants
Suppliers	Social Security	Travel
Travel	Taxes	Vital Papers
Warranties	Trusts	Warranties

COLOR CODING

Judy Thomson

Color coding for major file categories is a powerful tool for keeping files in order. Keep color coding as simple as possible. The purpose is to make it easy to remember what general category a folder belongs to, not to create a psychedelic delight.

Color coding can be done very inexpensively through the use of highlighters or colored pens; a bit more expensively using colored file labels, self-stick dots, or a combination of these. All these supplies come in a wide range of colors and are very versatile. Higher in cost are colored hanging folders and colored file folders. The choice is yours. Let your personal taste and pocketbook be your guide.

To color code an entire existing filing system in hanging files without replacing all the file folders, use colored tabs to identify categories. First, list all your different categories. Then choose colors that best represent the categories you have. This makes it easier to locate files and then to re-file them.

In addition to color coding entire filing systems, colored files can be used effectively to spotlight files for different reasons. You may want to highlight individual folders that need special attention or special handling: For example, in a sea of manila file folders, an insurance policy in a lime green folder can be spotted from across the room. You may also want to use specified colors for rush jobs, confidential files, unpaid bills, key accounts, or whatever material you need to be able to spot instantly.

Another use of color coding is to separate divisions and subjects within the office, even within one file drawer, for example: In an office where partners share clerical staff, each partner can be assigned a color so that everyone will always know at a glance whose files are whose. In a sales office where information is separated geographically, regions can be assigned distinguishing colors.

Colored file folders cost about $.23 each compared to $.15 for manila (the plain tan ones), but today's file folders can be labeled with removable labels and reused with ease. The steps and time saved by using a color code system may be well worth the investment.

MORE TIPS

✦ Keep extra file folders (and a folder stocked with appropriate labels only) at the front of each file drawer for easy access when creating a new file.

✦ Keep only the current year's records and other papers you need to refer to frequently in your files. Box up, label and store all other papers elsewhere.

✦ When folding legal-size papers to fit letter-size file folders, fold the extra length *away* from you underneath the rest of the page. Folding toward you covers the bottom inches of the page and requires you to unfold it to see it.

✦ Use removable file labels. They cost more but they redeem themselves in reusable file folders.

✦ Some types of papers (tax spreadsheets, articles, legal documents, business cards, mailing lists) may be more sensibly stored in three-ring binders than in your filing cabinet.

✦ When creating files, think "retrieval!" Don't ask "Where should I put this?" Ask "Where will I probably look when I want to find this again?"

✦ Keep file folders you use daily in the desk file drawer, filing can be done immediately and your most active files kept up to date easily. Files used only once a month should stay in the credenza or in a secondary work area near you. When you no longer use a particular file on a daily or frequent basis, move it out of the desk drawer and back into your regular file cabinet or storage.

✦ Background information, reference files, some administrative files that you need to access infrequently should be housed in the file cabinet or in a central file area in your office. It takes less time to walk out of your office and down the hall for a file you need occasionally than the time it takes to move it regularly in order to get to those you use more often.

✦ Label all files by using the subject to which the papers refer as the broad heading. For example, the *New York Times* article on "Managing Cultural Diversity" would be filed with other documents concerning cultural diversity but not under the headings of "newspaper articles," "articles" or "New York Times."

✦ Avoid creating a separate file for every type of document. Consolidate related materials under the most general category that is practical. This reduces the number of places to look for things.

✦ In your filing system, use both hanging file folders and interior file folders. By removing only the interior folders, the hanging file folders mark the place to which to return the file.

✦ As a general rule, never put more than three interior folders in a hanging file folder. If your files are stuffed, you will be less inclined to file or re-file papers; also, jammed files necessitate extracting the whole interior folder from the drawer just to get to one piece of paper. Filing systems that are easy to use, with extra room, are much more likely to be used regularly than file drawers that are overcrowded.

✦ To subdivide information within a file folder use a single, brightly colored piece of construction paper between sections. If a file is slim and likely to stay that way, a sticky note, labeled and folded back over the top of the pages of one section of information, will separate that section from the next. Put all sticky notes in the same spot relative to the papers—e.g., upper right corner.

✦ Buy sturdy file cabinets. If cost is a concern, look for used ones from office furniture stores, storage companies or classified ads. Spray paint can give new life to old cabinets and make them work with your office design. Beware, however, of jammed or sticky drawers. If a drawer is frustrating to use, or worse, painful or damaging to your body, you won't use it.

✦ When creating a filing system shared with others, use full names (no abbreviations) to develop a uniform system that others will be able to use easily and embellish as necessary. Stick to broad generic categories as headings.

✦ Use stick-on labels and neatly hand-write them with a dark permanent marker, or type them. Write the file title on the upper left corner and the major category (Finances, Personal, Clients, etc.) on the upper right. Add a description under the title on the lower right if needed, and indicate the pull date, if applicable. For the most effective files, use your own words for the titles.

✦ Place papers in a file with the top of the papers to the left of the file, so that when you open the file, its contents are ready to read like a book. Place the most recent papers on top so the file contents will be in chronological order and all oriented the same way in the file. Use staples rather than paper clips to keep articles together in the files. If you must clip papers together, clip them at the outside right edge, so the clips stay at the top edge of the file folder, so as not to bulge and tear the fold.

✦ If your files are bulging and you can't seem to find time to clean them all out, try doing the job in short, regular spurts. Fifteen minutes a day, regularly, can eliminate the problem. Another way is to clean dead wood out of each file folder when you open it.

✦ Be realistic, not idealistic. If you really just do not want to deal with setting up or overhauling a filing system, know that you are not alone, give yourself a hug and a smile, and hire a professional organizer! She can do a major office overhaul or a single closet or file drawer or project. You may also want to consider having your organizer return for a few hours or days on a regular basis to help you maintain your system.

✦ Shelf-life considerations for long-term filing and storage usually aren't mentioned when you buy a product. Until acid-free archival items become more the norm, it is worth noting a few products that do deteriorate over time:

Rubber bands. Broken pieces end up sticking to the surface they surround.

File folder labels last about four years with normal use. Some options are to buy plastic covers to place over labels, tape over the label with translucent tape (caution – see "Adhesive tape" below), or write directly on the file folder, bypassing labels altogether.

Fax paper will deteriorate very rapidly, within six months or a year. Photocopy faxes as soon as possible onto plain paper if you plan to save them.

Masking tape is meant for short-term projects only and will dry up, crack and chip off in pieces. Instead, use pushpins, nails or specially made adhesive strips for securing items.

Adhesive tape. What is true for masking tape is true for adhesive tape as well. Transparent adhesive tape, depending on the brand and situation, may also leave a sticky residue, stain or otherwise ruin the substance (e.g., a book binding) to which it adheres. Sticky debris is often removable with a cotton ball saturated with one of the all-purpose household sticky-debris-removers, available at the hardware store. But this won't always work. Even if it does, it may have some nasty side effects, such as removing a wood stain or finish, or soaking and demolishing a paper-based product.

Rubber cement eventually dries up. Before it does, it may darken the paper it's stuck to, which darkening can't be undone. In addition, papers long attached with rubber cement may be next to impossible to separate without tearing.

✦ Keep irreplaceable documents in a safe deposit box or a fire-proof box in your home. Keep photocopies of all these records in your filing system. These might include: wills, immunization records, stock certificates, household inventory, licenses (professional, pilots, etc.) passports, titles and deeds, appraisals, family genealogy, diplomas. Make a few extra copies of each so that they are available immediately when needed.

✦ Paper folders are not the only containers you can use to create filing systems. Similarly, file cabinets are not the only way to house "files." If your needs are simple (you don't own a business and just need to keep track of a few household records), a sturdy box or series of small boxes kept in a drawer or on a closet shelf may suffice. See the Containers chapter for other ideas.

14

GIFTS

"The more he gives to others, the more he possesses of his own."

— Lao Tzu

10 TIPS FOR CREATIVE GIFT GIVING
Lillian Vernon

1. Think carefully all year long about what people really want, and write down ideas as they come to mind.

2. Keep a list, and whenever you come across something on it, shop early, even if it's not near Christmas.

3. Start a gift hide-away and buy a little at a time. This will save you from having to do all your shopping at the last minute.

4. Start wrapping gifts as you get them so you won't have to wrap them all at once—you'll have more time to enjoy the holidays.

5. Buy decorative baskets or tins and fill them with soaps, potpourri, candies or homemade cookies.

105

6. Sentimental gifts can be very meaningful and fun too. Put old family photos in beautiful frames.

7. Write your family history in a bound book. It will be treasured for generations.

8. Create a special event—a luncheon, dinner, theater outing or a day spent together, a gift of yourself.

9. Use ornaments as gift tie-ons, especially personalized ones. They will delight everyone who receives one.

10. For a gift that won't fit under the tree, like a bicycle, paste a picture of it into a card or box.

GIFT GIVING
Kathryn Bechen

I keep a master list of people I buy gifts for throughout the year. When I spot a good sale, I buy an item, tag it with the person's name, make a note of the purchase on the list, and then store the gift until it's time to give it.

Storing the gifts in a handy organizer with cubbyholes makes it easy to see each person's name for quick identification. The shelves can be organized alphabetically by person or holiday, or numerically by birthdate, anniversary, etc.

15

GOALS

"If you don't know where you're going, you'll probably end up somewhere else."

— Yogi Berra

THE FREEDOM OF LIMITATIONS
Anacaria Myrrha

As we move through the 1990's, riding high on the edge of the Information Age, we find ourselves in an era of unlimited possibilities. We have access to more information than at any other time in history. We receive daily communications from all over the world, many of them contradictory. We receive offers on radio and television, in the mail and in the mall, most of them unrealistic.

We are exhorted to purchase, to consume, to give, to join. We are offered beauty, status, riches and pleasure. We are told that with the right toothpaste, designer suits and FAX machines, we will acquire power, success and love. The message is, whatever we can imagine, we can have . . . somehow.

In my opinion, human beings are not well suited to unlimited possibilities. Living without boundaries on a daily basis produces anxiety, frustration, and insecurity. Without a clear definition of how we choose to spend our time, we fall prey to every interesting outside stimuli, and are easily caught in the "webb" and flow of the urgent but not important. We are spread too thin, we regularly perform crisis management, and "everything" never gets done.

Recreation becomes another thing "to do" and is quickly canceled when deadlines demand. We get to rest if we get the flu. And spending time doing nothing is often viewed as suspicious if not downright immoral. Even when we manage to steal a few minutes or a few hours for ourselves, we are pursued by anxiety and guilt. When all options are constantly available, little can be accomplished in depth or with a sense of well being, and over a period of time depression and exhaustion often result.

When I sit with clients as they look over their lists and schedules, struggling to select their priorities, I realize that our choices are no longer between good and bad, want and don't want, or even better and best. Most of the things we want *are* the best, but are simply too much and too many for a single lifetime.

I have concluded that we can derive satisfaction and contentment from our lives only if we set limits for ourselves. If they are natural and comfortable, compassionate and realistic, they will produce results and will be easy to endure. If they arise from a value system which honors those things which fulfill us in the deepest sense of our being, they will inspire us and bring us joy.

The paradox is that by choosing limits, we can experience a measure of freedom not possible when all possibilities are constantly available.

THE IMPORTANCE OF SETTING GOALS
Tudi Baskay

What freeway do you take when you don't know where you're going? When do you start if you don't know how long it takes to get there? What do you take with you when you don't know what you're going to do?

People who would never think of starting on a vacation by getting on the nearest freeway think nothing of going through their days without ever thinking of where they want to be by nightfall.

To do a good job of goal setting and avoid the confusion and stress of disorganization, it is important to set both long- and short-term goals. Long-term goals serve as milestones on the horizon six months, a year, five years from now. They provide the context in which the entire spectrum of your life gets lived day by day, week by week, month by month.

Short-term goals define interim stops on the way to long-term goal achievement, which we can use to measure our progress toward the horizon. Setting long-term goals first, enables you to evaluate whether your short-term goals will really get you where you want to go. Short-term goals enable you to experience the satisfaction of producing results sooner rather than later. Short-term goals also make planning the present time-frame of today or this week much easier.

The tasks that show up on your daily To Do lists, weekly agendae and in monthly tickler files will reflect the steps you must take enroute to the short-term goals you define. Your list of long-term goals can be used most effectively as a reminder of your ultimate destination. To keep your perspective sharp, be sure you review your long-term goals frequently. Above all, be ready to revise your goals as you notice that your values change.

The purpose of writing down goals is to enable you to see whether the road you are traveling will take to get you where you want to go. Once you know what your goal is, you have a valuable guideline that assists in setting priorities and organizing your time.

MORE TIPS

✦ It's very helpful when you begin any project—especially a project like getting organized—to focus on the reasons why you set the goal and took on the project in the first place. Write down not only your goals, but your motivations and the payoffs that await you at completion of the journey. Share them with a buddy. Both actions will help you stay focused.

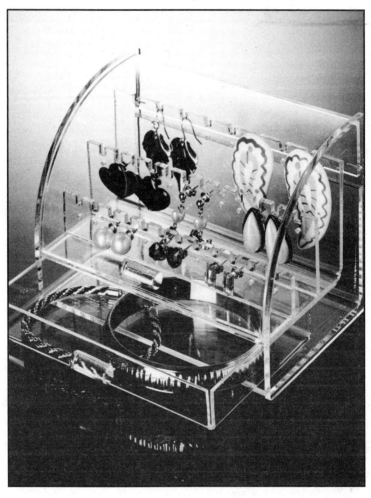

16

JEWELRY

"Adornment is never anything except a reflection of the heart."

— Coco Chanel

ORGANIZING YOUR JEWELRY
Christine Layer

Give away those fancy cloth-lined jewelry boxes that take up room on the dresser! Stop using earring ladders that just collect dust! Pick up those earrings and bracelets scattered about the room!

To store your jewelry in the most efficient manner possible you will want to purchase a small plastic storage cabinet—one with clear mini-drawers which will enable you easily to identify your jewelry pieces. These cabinets are generally advertised for storing nuts and bolts and are available at hardware stores. Since the cabinets come with various drawer sizes, choose one appropriate to the type and amount of jewelry you own, and leave room for likely expansion. These storage cabinets can stand alone or be wall-mounted, usually cost under $25 and come in many attractive colors, such as teal, blue and red.

Now the fun begins! All you need to do is separate your jewelry pieces into categories and then place them in the various drawers. The range of categories to choose from are limited only by your imagination and your collection. The following suggestions should help you get started.

- Divide jewelry by type: earrings, bracelets, anklets, necklaces, pins, rings.

- Divide each type of jewelry into smaller subdivisions. Some examples: composition (gold, silver, other metals), texture (cloth, beads, etc.), same-color tones and thematic or holiday pieces.

- Place in individual drawers the following items: watches, watches and bracelets frequently worn together, costume or party jewelry.

- Valuable pieces of jewelry can either be kept encased in soft cloth pouches in one drawer or stored separately in a hidden location.

- Designate one drawer as the fix-it drawer. Occasionally pins are missing beads or bracelets and necklaces have broken clasps. By keeping these items together you can repair them assembly-line style when you have time. It's recommended that you also store in this drawer a small pair of long/needle nose pliers, excellent for fixing broken jewelry and any other equipment (beading supplies, silicone cement) you use just for this purpose .

KEEPING VALUABLE JEWELRY
SECURE FROM THEFT

Hester Lox

Don't store all your valuables in one place. *Do* remember where you've stored each piece. Write it down, if you have to, in a simple code that is clear to you but won't be an obvious treasure map to a burglar. For example, the costly cameo my mother brought me from Florence, Italy lives in the pocket of a pink bathrobe I never wear. My list simply says "pink Florence."

Small valuables can be hidden in containers that are falsely labeled to look like ordinary products—a light timer box is my mom's favorite (but I won't tell you where she lives). You can purchase name brand "products" that are actually cans (soups, sodas or sprays) hollowed out and lined for this purpose. These are available at hardware and packaging stores, among others. A caveat here: keep track of what's what. A recent news report told of a kind woman who gave four cans of tomato soup to a charity food drive, only to discover to her horror a week later that she had unwittingly donated her grandmother's wedding ring and a lock from her daughter's first haircut as well.

It's a good idea to photograph your jewelry periodically. In case of an insurance claim after a burglary or natural disaster, the photos may prove extremely valuable. Store the photos in your safe deposit box.

MORE TIPS

✦ Use drawer organizer boxes to hold earrings, watches, and necklaces in the bathroom, bedroom or closet.

115

✦ A panty hose organizer with small plastic pockets will hold many necklaces.

✦ Plastic hooks with adhesive backs can be purchased at hardware and discount stores. Line them up on the wall in a closet, bathroom or dressing area to hold necklaces and beads.

✦ A desk organizer tray with divided sections will hold an assortment of different jewelry.

✦ Put special jewelry into a safe deposit box, fireproof box or at least a waterproof and dust proof plastic box. Keep your every day jewelry more accessible.

✦ Fragile or complex earrings, pins and brooches can be attached to a length of cloth, a hand towel, or a washcloth. Roll carefully to use this as an inexpensive, padded jewelry holder when traveling.

✦ Separating jewelry into little baskets that stack makes it easy to find the piece you want in your jewelry drawer.

✦ Store earrings in cylindrical, clear plastic boxes used for fishing flies. Each section screws together, one on top of the other, and can be stored either upright on a shelf or lying down in a drawer. To make the compartments more elegant, each can be lined with a circle of felt or ultra suede cut to size.

From the Lillian Vernon Catalog

17
KITCHENS

"But, lady, as women, what wisdom may be ours if not the philosophies of the kitchen? Lupercio Leonardo spoke well when he said: How well one may philosophize when preparing dinner. And I often say when observing these trivial details: had Aristotle prepared victuals, he would have written more."

— Juana Ines de la Cruz

KEEPING KITCHEN
INFORMATION ORGANIZED
Annie Rohrbach

Put a small filing cabinet or file drawer in your kitchen or wherever you do your meal planning. It's the perfect place for keeping recipes, diet and nutrition information, appliance instructions and warranties, and other household-care-related items. If you have the room, also add plans, instructions and ideas for household plants, your garden, interior and holiday decorating, shopping lists, sale catalogs, ads, etc. This keeps your home office area less cluttered and free for such things as correspondence, financial planning, bill paying and other paperwork.

Organize all those recipes clipped from magazines and newspapers into two separate sections: Recipes to Try, and Tested Recipes to Keep. Use the same titles for the dividers for both systems (appetizers, breads, etc.) so it is easy to transfer those you like into your permanent files. Throw away recipes that don't appeal to you.

Create an Entertainment file to keep track of menus and recipes you serve for company. It's a great source for future ideas and also helps you keep track of what you have served to whom .

MORE TIPS

✦ Keep similar things together in cabinets and drawers: baking items, pots, skillets, cutlery, etc.

✦ Keep knives in safe order by wedging a heavy metal spring into a drawer, then insert a knife in the space between each coil.

✦ Hang frequently used pots or pans directly over the stove within easy reach.

✦ Store all cleaning supplies (including paper towels and dust rags) in one pail which you can carry with you from room to room as you clean. If you use different supplies for different rooms, use more than one pail and divide supplies accordingly.

✦ Wad up plastic grocery bags and stuff them into empty paper towel rolls for storage. This recycles both items and keeps them neat and accessible.

✦ Store all items as close as possible to the area where they are used. For instance, pots, pans, spatulas, labels next to or under the stovetop. Silverware, napkins and placemats near the dining area.

✦ Put dry goods (cereal, rice, flower, etc.) into sealed, clear plastic containers. This keeps them visible and allows you to stack them to take advantage of "dead space" at the top of cabinet shelves. Be sure to label the containers for easy identification.

✦ Mini laundry baskets (6-1/2" x 8") are great for holding packaged powder mixes (taco seasonings, soup and gravy mixes, pudding and gelatin, etc.), which can be alphabetized,

✦ Mini laundry baskets also make great containers for pan lids, strainers and other kitchen tools.

✦ Use a dry-erase board inside a kitchen cabinet for an ongoing grocery list. Whenever you run low on something, put it on the list. Don't erase the item until the it has been purchased.

✦ Store rolls of foil, plastic wrap and various sizes of plastic bags that come packaged in boxes into a sturdy plastic sweater storage container in one kitchen cabinet. Slide it out like a drawer to reach for the box you want.

Alternative Ways to Store Spices.

✦ Arrange spices in alphabetical order. Then you know what you have and the exact location.

✦ Arrange spices by category: leaf herbs in one rack; seeds in another; pie spices such as cinnamon and cloves in a third; pepper, dry mustard and curry in a fourth, and the things you only use in special recipes in the last.

✦ Put spices and herbs together by frequency of use, keeping the ones you use regularly near your cooking area. Store the others at the back of a cabinet.

✦ Store the spices you actually use in a drawer next to the stove, and throw the rest away.

From the Lillian Vernon Catalog

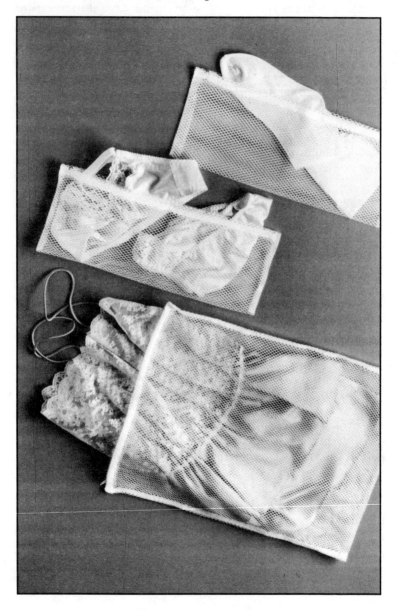

18
LAUNDRY

"You can't get spoiled if you do your own ironing!"

— Meryl Streep

DESIGN AN EFFICIENT LAUNDRY SYSTEM
Kathleen Poer

If your household is comprised of two or more people, preteen and older, the total number of hours spent collecting, sorting, washing, drying, folding and putting away the household laundry each week can equal the better part of a day! This need not be the responsibility of one person—namely you—alone. A system of teamwork combined with a well-designed laundry area will make everyone's life easier and happier.

As with any system, however, it must be simple, well-designed and attractive to encourage use. Consider a design similar to this one suggested for a designer's showcase:

The System

Responsibility is divided among household members. Each person collects his own laundry in his own bag (which is conveniently hung on the back of his closet door) or in his closet system basket. Every few days, each person carries his laundry to the laundry room and sorts it into the correct baskets (conveniently marked by type of wash load).

As baskets become full, a load can be washed and dried accordingly. Be sure to do this when there will be time to fold any clothes that need to be folded right from the dryer. Save the others for when you are baking a pie or doing another activity with built-in "waiting time." Any item that needs to drip dry or be ironed can be hung right from the dryer on a nearby hanger.

Rather than carry all the clean clothes to each person, instruct everyone to check the laundry area periodically for their own things (either hanging or in a basket). Removal of clean stuff from this area ASAP will prevent confusion. Towels and sheets can go directly from bathrooms and beds to the laundry and back.

Materials Needed

- **Tubular plastic hangers**, color-coded for each person.
- **Laundry bags** for each person's closet (or a basket within a closet system).
- **A basket system** to serve as a sorting area. You'll need a minimum of four rectangular baskets. Label them according to the way you sort your loads, remembering to provide easy identification for children, for example, Whites, Delicates (permanent press), Pants & T-shirts (dark cottons and blends) and Special (anything that doesn't fit in the other categories).
- **Shelving**
- **A hanging system.** An over-the-door hanger works well in a laundry. If your area is in the garage, hang a wooden dowel from the rafters.

How to Design the Space

The installation of your washer and dryer will be your starting point. (To economize on room space, use stacked appliances.) Your laundry area might take shape in the garage or in a utility room. A more spacious area could also do double duty as a hobby area.

Install shelving above and/or to the side of your washer/dryer combination to hold laundry soaps, etc. Several manufacturers make laundry shelf systems that provide hanging capability for items you need to drip dry or iron. Or you can install one of the hanging systems mentioned above.

Install the basket system along a wall near the washer, or in the center of the work area. A laminated plastic top placed on the system can serve as a surface for folding clothes. In a larger space, consider having a work island built and slide the basket system under the countertop. Baskets can be used for more than the sorting of laundry; they can also be used to transport clean items back to the bedrooms.

Store a folding ironing board against the wall on a specially designed hanger; or invest in a wall-mounted model or one that is installed in a drawer.

MORE TIPS

✦   Keep those empty paper towel and gift paper rolls. After ironing, or right from the dryer, roll napkins, table cloths, runners, etc., around the rolls. This keeps them from creasing while in a drawer or closet.

✦   Recycling bins make great laundry room helpers for sorting clothes going to different rooms of the house or to different family members.

125

✦   When dealing with limited space (such as in a studio or one-bedroom apartment), a clothesline across two hooks mounted above either end of the bathtub serves as an ideal place to hang wet clothes.

✦   Tie a knot in legs of panty hose that are slightly snagged so that when laundered they can be easily identified for wearing with slacks.

19
MAIL ORDER

"During the month of June I acted as a Pony Express rider carrying the U.S. mail between Deadwood and Custer, a distance of 50 miles.... It was considered the most dangerous route in the Hills, but as my reputation as a rider and quick shot was well known, I was molested very little, for the toll gatherers looked on me as being a good fellow, and they knew I never missed my mark."

— Martha Jane Burke, a.k.a. Calamity Jane

ORDERING BY MAIL
Beth Blair

Do you know that you have additional protection and recourse if you mail rather than phone your order to a company? To save yourself time and headaches later, do the following:

Fill out the order form completely and legibly. Photocopy the order before you mail it. When the merchandise arrives, inspect the package. Make sure any damage is noted before the delivery person leaves. (You can refuse delivery with most freight carriers if you feel it's necessary.) On the shipping form, write down the date the package arrived. If you need to make a return, photocopy the completed return form. Then ship the package (using the original container if possible) via an insured carrier. Keep the return documentation in your Pending file until the replacement arrives or the credit or refund appears.

MORE TIPS

✦ To remove your name from mailing lists, send a postcard every six months to:

Mail Preference Service
Direct Mail Marketing Association
P.O. Box 9008
Farmingdale, NY 11735-9008

This company is a list broker and mail order house. Ask them to remove your name from all their lists. This will cut down considerably the amount of fourth class mail you receive.

✦ Save space, save money. If you only infrequently need to use a postal scale, make your own as needed. Put a 12-inch ruler on a pencil so it's centered over the 6-inch mark. Place five quarters (1 ounce) on the 3-inch mark. Center your sealed envelope on the 9-inch mark . If the quarters don't move you know your letter is under one ounce.

20
MOVING

"Three moves are worse than a fire!"

— Grandma Agnes Smith

HONEST TO GOODNESS TIPS FOR A SMOOTH MOVE
Linda J. Lipton

Moving is a stressful (with a capital S!) time. However, there are things you can do to make your move and your life easier.

Having consulted with professional movers, I've learned some of the most common mistakes that people make in the process of preparing to move, and how *you* can avoid making them.

Mistake #1: Not having a layout plan prepared for the new location. If you're tempted to think it will all come together on its own, you're deceiving yourself. It won't. Preplanning is probably the most important part of an efficient move. Even more important, it facilitates the settling-in process once you're in your new home. If at all possible, get a floor plan of your new home. It will help you visualize how your belongings will fit. It would be great if you could have an actual layout to-scale (1/4" = 1') that shows where your furnishings are to be placed. At the very least, have some kind of organizational chart that

131

includes a list of your furnishings with their room designations. It's to your advantage also to designate closet and cabinet contents. The more preplanning you can do, the better. And of course, share all of this information with your mover.

Mistake #2: Bringing into your new home more than is necessary right away. This may seem to contradict mistake #1, but the two actually go hand in hand. Preplanning enables you to determine your essentials, and have your boxes labeled accordingly. Use your garage or spare bedroom to store nonessential boxes and items. Unpacking takes time, even in an organized fashion. It's important to have some livable space during this overwhelming process. (Packing immediate-necessity items is addressed below.)

Mistake #3: Not having access to essentials because they're buried somewhere in your boxes. Pack a survival box or two. Include instant beverages, cups, paper towels, toilet paper, cleansing soap, a first aid kit, any daily medications, your child's favorite toy, one set of linens and blankets for each bed and, basically, whatever you think you'll need to get by temporarily.

Mistake #4: Packing boxes too heavily; using boxes that are too large. Be aware of this. It slows the process down if you need more than one pair of hands to move a box, and may cause physical damage to the contents, or injury to the humans.

Mistake #5: Using improper packing or packaging materials. It's best to use regulation moving boxes. They're uniform and made to hold up under rough handling. Uniformity makes for quicker, safer handling, thus saving you time and money. Damaged or tired boxes may not hold up in the move and are likely to cause spillage and damage to your goods.

Do not use printed newspaper. The ink can stain your items. When combined with the natural oils of your fingers, it can leave permanent fingerprints on whatever you touch. This is especially true for china which has some porosity. It's worth the investment to get proper packaging materials from your mover or from a professional packaging supplier. The job will go faster and cleaner!

If economics are a serious consideration, procure at least enough plain wrapping paper to use as the first layer of cushion next to your possessions, and use newspaper only for the outer layers. When unpacking, unwrap all the newsprint first, then wash the ink off your hands before you unwrap the plain paper layer.

Plates are less likely to break if they are packed standing on edge. Minimize breakage of glass items by placing the heavier ones on the bottom and the more delicate ones on top. Even better is to obtain a "dish pack" from your movers, or have them pack your breakables – they're professionals. If *you* pack your own breakables, then they generally are *not* covered by the moving company's liability policy.

Artwork framed with acrylic should not be wrapped in paper, which will scratch the surface. It's best to use polystyrene foam available at packaging stores, some framing and art supply stores, or from your movers.

Mistake #6: Ignoring the physical limitations and legal restrictions of the neighborhood regarding large vehicles, unloading, etc. Check with local authorities and make sure that your mover is also aware of access limitations at your destination. It is your mover's responsibility to provide you with an access plan that addresses any restrictions, and let you know how they will be dealt with. Make sure your mover lives up to that responsibility. In doing so you will spare yourself a potential nightmare situation.

Mistake #7: Overlooking the fine print on your moving contract. This is especially true regarding the liability of the moving company concerning damage to your possessions. The standard coverage may actually cover only a small percentage of the value of your goods. (Sixty cents per pound is standard. Thus, a TV weighing 50 lbs. would be covered for $30.) Work out the legal liability with your mover *before the move* and understand exactly what your coverage is. Additional coverage can be expensive. Find out if your homeowner's insurance has a rider that covers moves. If it does, it is probably less expensive and more complete than what your mover can provide.

Mistake #8: Undervaluing your own time, energy and resources. Consider how much of your time you may spend running around to locate packing materials, small truck rentals, etc. Include the cost of gas for your car, as well your labor. It may be worth your while to hire specialists to work with you and for you. Do not undervalue service or conscientiousness.

Mistake #9: Being intimidated by your movers; not communicating your needs. Your movers are working *for you*. They are handling *your* belongings. Quality movers welcome your questions and concerns and appreciate working out the details with you. In selecting a mover, a comfortable rapport, sense of responsibility and service orientation are as important, if not more so, than price. If you have the time, go see the mover's trucks and equipment. Notice how the company's employees present themselves. Appearance means a lot. Get a list of recommendations from the moving company, and call a few of the names. You can also check with the Public Utilities Commission to find out if there is any record of complaint, and if the mover's license is valid.

PACKING TIPS FOR YOUR MOVE
by Johanna Luther

Packing is a chore that most people hate. Here are ten hints to help you pack so that everything will arrive safely at your new home.

1. Organize the move in your mind. Make a mental room by room inventory of your possessions. Include the garage and all storage areas. Then make a written list noting the number of boxes you think will be needed for each area.

2. Start procuring boxes early. An average three-bedroom house will require 70 boxes or more. Use small boxes for heavy things like books and records. Use medium boxes for pots, pans, small appliances, toys. Reserve large boxes for linens, blankets, pillows, lamp shades.

3. Gather your packing materials. You will need carton sealing tape, marking pens, masking tape, labels (large, white self-adhesive and "fragile"), bubble wrap, packing peanuts, newspaper, plain white newsprint for wrapping dishes and fragile items.

4. Start packing early. Six weeks prior to the move is not too soon. Begin with areas not frequently used: basement, attic, highest closet shelves. Pack a few boxes each day or whenever you have some extra time. Schedule several days just before the move for final packing.

5. Clearly label each box on its top or on its right front corner. Indicate on the label where the box is to go. List the general contents on the label. Number each box on the label and enter that number on a master log of boxes. On the master log list the detailed contents of each box. (This step may seem unnecessary but it will save much confusion when the boxes arrive at your new address.)

6. Take special care with fragile items. Use double-walled boxes for dishes, glasses and fragile items. Wrap fragile things first in white paper and then bubble wrap. Pack all your boxes full and fill up any air space with crumpled newspaper or packing peanuts. Label or clearly mark boxes "fragile."

7. Nest your lampshades. Tape a masking tape note to the wire frame on each shade to indicate to which lamp it belongs.

Wrap the light bulbs in bubble wrap, put them inside a paper bag with a note indicating to which lamps the bulbs belong. Pack bulbs with the lampshades. Fill the remaining space in the box with packing peanuts.

8. Put your refrigerator items in a picnic cooler. Pack the freezer items together. Tighten all tops and lids. Transfer everything immediately into your new refrigerator.

9. Make special arrangements for pets, plants and children. Pets should be put in a quiet room at the new location until the movers have gone. Remember to give them food, water, a litter box and reassurance. Plants don't do well in moving vans. Carry them in your car. Children need special attention on moving day. A caring relative or friend who can be there just for them will help smooth the transition.

10. Recycle all your packing materials. Have on hand large plastic garbage bags to collect the packing debris. Sort the crumpled paper, bubble wrap and packing peanuts. Break down the boxes and bundle them for recycling. Arrange for curbside pickup or plan a trip to a recycling center.

21
PAPER

"What the world really needs is more love and less paper work."

— Pearl Bailey

PAPER: WHEN TO TOSS IT
AND WHEN TO SAVE IT
Odette Pollar

When to Toss

Just because you could conceivably use it under the right circumstances, at the right time, sometime between now and your funeral is not a valid reason to save a piece of paper. You cannot keep everything just because it is interesting.

How can you determine what is safe to toss? Here are some guidelines:

- Is it a *duplicate*?
- What is the *date*?
- Do I *need* this or simply *want* this? Why?
- *How often* will I refer to the information?
- Is the information *current and relevant* to my work or life?
- Will it add something *new* to the material already on hand?

137

- Do I have the *time* to read this?
- Does *someone else* have this information?
- How *likely* am I to need to refer to it again?

When To Save

- It is the only copy.
- Replication would be very difficult.
- You will need to refer to the information again soon.
- You are required by law to keep it.
- It is an integral part of the client or project file.

HOW TO USE BUSINESS CARDS EFFECTIVELY
Eve Laraine Abbott

Always carry your business cards with you. Nearly everyone you meet is a potential client or may need a referral to another business. People who benefit from a referral you have given them remember your business too!

You can double the effective impact of your business card by having the reverse side printed with highlights of your products or services (or a quote from a satisfied client illustrating your specialty).

Use your business card as your name tag. Keep a plastic name tag holder with you for networking occasions. Remember, networking can take place at any kind of meeting: hobby, politics, computer swap, crafts fair, etc. People who share your interests are more likely to use your services.

When you meet someone and accept her card, make a note on the card about any outstanding impression that the person or the business made on you, as well as where and when you met.

Choose a type of address file that accommodates business cards. If you use a rotary card file, transfer your notes to the back of the card to which the business card is stapled.

Use your specific notes on the new contact's business card to personalize a follow-up mailing to introduce your business.

When you send correspondence, attach your business card with a small self-adhesive sticker. The card can be removed from the stationery without damage. Apply your business card to your brochures at networking events, as well.

Remember to use your business card in any kind of communication. This saves time, eliminates errors and can be a conversation starter. Every person in business uses other businesses, and your card makes it easy for them to refer others to you.

MORE TIPS

✦   For keeping track of personal correspondence, keep a daily, dated journal of things done, Nobel prizes received, appointments and letters written. You then have record of who you wrote to when, plus a record of everything that happened from the time you last wrote.

✦   Throw out junk mail immediately, the first time you go through your mail.

✦   If you have a post office box, discard all your junk mail immediately, right there at the post office!

✦ There are basically only four things you can do with a piece of paper: toss it, file it, delegate it or act on it yourself. To deal with incoming mail efficiently, have a wastebasket and three files or trays ready and put each piece of paper in the appropriate place. Then process each category in turn.

✦ Handle paper only once at each stage of its progress: once to sort, once to deal with, and once to file, pass on to someone else or throw away.

✦ Suggested work flow boxes for home offices: when you bring in the mail or bring things home from work, immediately sort the items, into either the trash or one of four workflow boxes: To Do, Pending, Reading, or Filing. Use the following criteria for determining what goes into each box:

To Do: All items which need action. These should be put in priority order as you add new items.

Pending: Items needing additional information or action for completion. These should be kept in alphabetical order. Once the information needed is received, either complete the work or put it into the To Do box.

Reading: Material which you must or want to read. Make sure you schedule specific time in your calendar for reading. Once read, either throw it out or put it in the Filing box.

Filing: Completed items which must be kept. Make sure you schedule specific time in your calendar for filing.

✦ Suggested workflow boxes for commercial offices:

In: This box is for your secretary, messenger or co-workers, in which to leave things for you. From your In box, distribute your incoming work: To Do, Pending, Reading and Filing.

Out: This box is for items which will be picked up and distributed by or for you, such as letters to be typed and outgoing mail. Unless a third box (To Central Filing) is used also, put files to be returned to the central office filing system in this box for pick-up.

To Central Filing: This box is only for files and papers that are to be filed in the central office filing system.

22
PETS

"If a fish is the movement of water embodied, given shape, then cat is a diagram and pattern of subtle air."

— Doris Lessing

"To call him a dog hardly seems to do him justice, so in as much as he had four legs, a tail, and barked, I admit he was to all outward appearances. But to those of us who knew him well he was a perfect gentleman."

— Hermione Gingold

BE A RESPONSIBLE PET OWNER
Hester Lox

A pet is a living, breathing miracle of nature, just like you. It will be totally dependent on you to meet many of its needs for its entire life. Are you prepared to provide more than adequate food and shelter, clean up after it, teach it (if its an animal that interacts with people or other animals), pay for its medical care (this can be substantial), be its life companion (friendship is a two-way street), and let it go when its time has come? Think seriously about these issues before buying or adopting a pet. If you cannot answer yes to every one of these questions, then the time is not right for you to become the guardian of an animal.

If you *are* an animal's guardian, *please* have your pet spayed or neutered. There are 1,001 reasons for not doing this:

"She's really pretty."
"She should have at least one heat so she's not frustrated."
"I want the kids to experience the miracle of birth."
"I paid a fortune for him and I want to recoup my investment on the siring fee."

These reasons crumble miserably in the face of the real-life catastrophe of unwanted pets that end up being euthanized every day in animal shelters. Of all the waste that human beings create, this is truly one of the saddest kinds. Be part of the solution.

MORE TIPS

✦ If you use a bag for food, use a clip (intended for chips) on the top of the dog food bag to keep it fresh and to keep it from spilling. Binder clips also work well for this purpose.

✦ An 18-gallon bin is just the right size to hold a 40 lb. bag of dry dog food.

✦ Put the dog's bowl of water inside a slightly larger bowl to catch the spills that always seem to happen.

✦ To curb the enthusiasm of a dog that jumps up onto visitors' laps uninvited, train the dog early that lap-sitting is only permitted if you have a towel on your lap. Keep one rolled up in a cupboard in the living room and/or family room so that when you want the dog on your lap, the "signal" is easily accessible.

✦ Make a Pet Center in a convenient spot in the house. Keep all your pet's medication, brushes, collars, extra dishes, toys, etc. in a basket or box together in this spot.

✦ Hang leashes and collars for pets near the door (or on hooks on the door).

✦ Small caged critters: Shredded paper is much less messy than wood chips, and the price is right. Stick to porous paper (computer, business or news); avoid the glossy, colored stuff used in advertising flyers and magazines. Your local animal shelter may have a shredder and happily donate bags of it to you. (Bring your own bags. Plastic is best, so you can tie the handles into a loose knot for convenience in transport and storage). Many business offices also create this kind of waste and may be willing to let you have some.

✦ A little creativity can save both money and the environment. Instead of buying prepackaged soft bedding for my rat, he gets small (about three inches square) pieces of clean natural fabric from T-shirt collars or too-long pants legs. He immediately turns these into blankets and privacy walls.

23

PHOTOGRAPHS

"The camera is an instrument that teaches people how to see without a camera."

— Dorothea Lange

HOW TO ORGANIZE
YOUR PHOTOGRAPHS

Lee Victoria Larsen

I take pictures of just about every event I'm involved in, so I am qualified to discuss the various options of how to organize photos. After I had my baby and built our house, I wound up with boxes of photos without labels or notes and in some cases, not even dates! So, out of necessity more than scholarly interest in how to expand my organizing expertise, I have developed these options for dealing successfully with photographs and feeling good about it throughout the various stages.

First, a few basics of photo handling are in order.

I highly recommend automatically ordering duplicate prints. With the exception of one-hour developers, a full set of duplicates is usually less costly than several reprints where special handling of negative strips is involved. Also, this eliminates the confusion later when your reprints finally come in and it's difficult to remember which print is for whom! Then, there's the maddening challenge of trying to return the negative strips to the original set, or worse, trying to find the same negatives later and not remembering what kind of envelope to look for.

Designate an accessible box, drawer, oversized envelope or archival container for this year's photos. This eliminates desktop photo clutter, and makes retrieving a photo easier.

As years pass, photos lose their meaning when no written information accompanies them. Therefore, the following three options center around how notes regarding your photos are made:

1. Put your photos into albums as soon as you receive them. This could save the step of labeling the back of each photo if your scrapbook includes informative notes. However, only an elite few actually accomplish this feat.

2. Label each photo as soon as you pick them up from developing. Include the event, date, name(s) of people and/or location. The liberating aspect of this option is that if several years pass before you actually assemble your scrapbook, the key data will still be at your fingertips. This will make the album assembly flow smoothly and allow it to be creative and even fun!

3. Label each envelope of prints with the key events, dates, names and locations. In addition, it can be helpful to number the envelopes sequentially within each year (1994/1, 1994/2, 1994/3).

If you work with option number two or three above, then assembling your album will come later. When that auspicious day arrives, maximize your time with this sequence of activities:

1.   Begin with a major sort. Group stacks of each event and use sticky notes, which can later serve as interim written entries in your album.

2.   Bravely weed out duplicates and photos which are either inferior in quality or very similar to others of the same subject.

3.   Keep a supply of envelopes handy as you sort the give-away photos. As you think of a likely recipient, immediately write her name on an envelope and slip in the photo(s). Voila! They're just one step closer to being ready to mail.

4.   Refine the stacks of photos that you created from the major sort and place them in chronological order.

5.   Install photos in albums, page by page. If you are challenged with unlabeled photos from prior years, a helpful technique is to temporarily stick photos on top of loose-leaf photo album pages. Then, when you come across an entirely new stash of photos relating to this era, they can easily be integrated. When all photo stashes are purged, then transfer into permanent album pages.

Here are some final thoughts about organizing photos. Ultimately, this is for fun, nostalgia and a unique means of enhancing ties with family and friends. So, liberate from your collection photos that bring up negative feelings and decorate the ones which make your heart sing. Most importantly, rid yourself of any guilt you may experience that results from your accumulation of photos. Resolve to begin taking the few extra minutes each time your photos are developed to make notes, starting now! Then it does not matter how far into the future you may choose to wait to compile your albums; the pictures will be ready to tell their stories.

MORE TIPS

✦ Place your envelopes of negatives (labeled with date and contents) into a fire-proof box. Then if a disaster occurs, you are much more likely to be able to reprint your precious photos.

✦ Use acid-free paper, pens and albums to display photos. Their lifetime will be greatly extended.

✦ Keep duplicate photos together in a folder. That way they will be handy when you want to drop a few into a letter to relatives.

✦ Plan to take your film in to be developed the week you finish the roll.

✦ Order all reprints within one week of development. This will prevent loss of the negatives or confusion as to which roll that really great photo was on.

24
PLANNING

"I expect to spend the rest of my life in the future, so I want to be reasonably sure of what kind of future it's going to be."

— Charles Kettering

THE ART OF PLANNING
Scott Plakun

You've heard it many times: *Plan your work and work your plan.* The problem is that planning is such a bother. Too complicated. Takes too much time. Why plan when I already know what I'm doing? Wrong on all counts. Lets look:

Myth #1: Planning is too complicated. A lot of books have been written that make planning seem very complex, but it needn't be. Because they need to be general, books cover every possible planning wrinkle for the most complex situations. Odds are that your project isn't the most complex. And if it is, it's unlikely that you'll use every possible planning trick. So relax. Keep it simple. Write down what you need to do and when. Don't use a planning methodology that's fancier than your project.

Myth #2: Planning takes too much time. The usual approach to a project is to plunge in and not take time to plan until you run

153

into problems. Planning after the fact takes more time; you have to deal with all the problems! Plan first, and you'll avoid the problems altogether. You get back two to four minutes of execution time for every minute you spend planning.

Myth #3:   I already know what I'm doing. You probably do, when you stop and think about it. But when was the last time you stopped and thought about it? Most people tend to deal with what's right in front of them rather than what needs to be done. A written plan summarizes the most important parts of your project, in the most efficient order. So instead of wandering all over the planet on the way from here to there, you stay closer to the shortest path.

You can be winning but feel like you're losing if you're not keeping score. Nobody wants to feel like they're losing. But you can't keep score unless you know the rules. Use planning to define the rules and where you belong—in the winner's circle.

MENTAL ORGANIZATION FOR PROJECT SUCCESS
Jafra Austin

If your mind is overloaded with more project details than you can keep track of, give yourself a break and unload it. Clearing out mental clutter will restore to you the ability to give more efficient, higher-quality attention to your responsibilities.

One effective way I know to do this is with a personalized action form that you can use to keep track of tasks associated with individual projects in which you are involved until all the items on your list have been completed.

Start by making a list of the general categories (and sub-categories) of actions which you know from experience you are likely to be required to perform on a regular basis. You may not cover all the bases at first, so leave space at the bottom for tasks to be added later as they occur to you.

Make a few copies of your list and attach one to each incomplete project folder. Next, taking each project in turn, check each item on the action list that is applicable to that project.

If you are in a position to delegate any tasks, you may want to have your forms printed up with carbonless duplicates, so you can note to whom you delegate actions and pass on to that person a copy of your form with appropriate instructions attached.

Your action form is also useful to help you prioritize your actions. You can color-code your check marks or emphasize items with highlighter pens so that your priorities will be obvious at a glance.

When an action has been completed, check it off. When the project is complete, file or store its materials together. It can be useful to file your completed action forms together in a notebook, so that over time you can see how the range of your actions changes, assess the items you added as "other," and revise your form as appropriate.

On the following page are some examples of categories and sub-categories that may suit your needs or remind you of the tasks you habitually do:

Task Categories

Call/contact _____	Request _____
Research with _____	Arrange for _____
Confirm with _____	Copy & mail/mail to _____
Make appointment to _____	Make appointment w/ ____
Prepare _____	Set up appointment _____
Meet with _____	Organize _____
Compile/organize _____	Compute _____
Follow up _____	Follow up with _____
Evaluate _____	Edit/complete _____

Waiting for _____ (especially useful for tracking materials slowed by red tape, such as government-related forms and certified documents)

THE IMPORTANCE OF ACKNOWLEDGEMENT

Robin Gurse

There are four crucial steps to the act of accomplishing: planning, doing, acknowledgment and rest. When any one of these is missing, we may experience feelings such as fear, apathy, shame or frustration, and end up procrastinating. One of these important steps is acknowledgment.

Most people I know who put off initiating or completing projects are not lazy or stupid or cowardly. They're unacknowledged. That is, they go from one task or project to another without pausing to actually reflect on what it was they did or did not do. The act of thinking or saying out loud, to ourselves or another person, allows us to "have" our accomplishment. When we are acknowledged, we don't get to discount, minimize, or deny our actions; rather, we get to tell the truth about them, create resolution and prepare ourselves for whatever is next. So take a moment or two—even ten seconds will do—and acknowledge your accomplishments.

Photo courtesy of Day Runner, Inc.

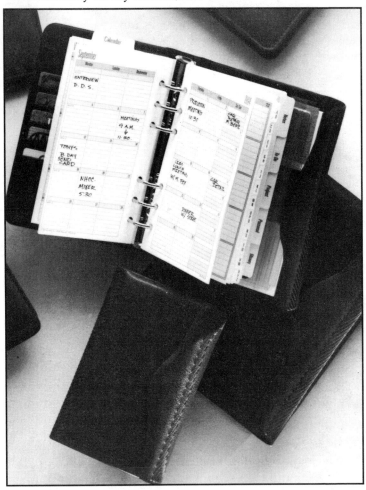

25
PLANNING
NOTEBOOKS

"Punctuality is the politeness of kings."

— Louis XVIII

WHAT TO LOOK FOR IN A
PERSONAL ORGANIZER NOTEBOOK
Scott Plakun

There are a lot of calendars and organizer notebooks out there. In fact, you see more of them every day. Although they all look the same on the outside, they vary greatly on the inside. Some are simple daily calendars. Others are calendars with extra sections to overcome the weaknesses of the calendar format. The best are organized around goals, projects and results rather than dates.

Many people use calendar-based personal organizers simply because they are used to them. But a results-oriented organizer/planner notebook can be much more effective.

Here's an overview of what to look for when you are shopping for a personal organizer notebook:

It's likely that the reason you are shopping for a new tool is because you want better results: improved time management, higher productivity and/or better personal organizational skills, so buying a new organizer notebook isn't enough. Improved results only come with changes in behavior.

Look for a product that includes training. With training you are sure to (1) understand the features and design of your system, and how to make them work for you and (2) get the motivation and information you need to increase your chances of making change successfully. A few products that include training offer money-back guarantees, obviously an advantage to you as the consumer.

Select a product designed to help you manage your whole life, professional and personal. Since there is only one of you, it works best to use just one personal management system (except that some people find that a combination of a paper-based notebook for the whole-life overview and a computer-based system for the details works best.)

The features you can expect to find in a well-designed product include:

Standard-sized pages with standard hole punches. This seems like a small thing, but using a notebook that isn't designed for paper sizes that are standard in the country where you live will create many problems. A binder with more than three rings requires that you either purchase a special hole punch or carefully punch each hole in each page you add to the notebook.

A separate appointment management section. Appointments are commitments that you make with one or more people (including yourself). A dedicated appointment manager helps you build your days around those commitments so you don't disappoint anybody. You don't need much room for each day; a larger space will only encourage you to build in more appointments. Most people can successfully handle only four to six appointments per day. A month-at-a-glance format works best.

A separate activities management section. Keeping your list of action items organized by day, broken down by month, provides a powerful tickler system for daily and long-range planning. The activities list should include an indication of the relative importance (priority) of each item, along with an action date to tell you when the item needs your attention.

Effective daily planning tools. A good notebook system should be designed so you create a new plan each day, working from the appointments and activities managers. Because things almost always move at a speed different from what you expect, building a daily plan too far in advance generates confusion and difficulty. The daily plan form should include an area for your appointments, a prioritized action list with time estimates, an area to record expenses and mileage, and a place for brief notes. The overall design should make planning simple. If you need to spend more than 15 minutes planning, there's something wrong.

Communications tracking tools. What gives results-oriented systems their added power is the practice of keeping your plans and notes organized by subject rather than date. Each project you're working on—and each person you're in communication with—should have its own note page where you document your plans and your actions. The activities manager should function as an index and tickler for these notes. While some products come with a whole library of specialized tracking forms, you'll likely find that the one general-purpose form is easier to deal with.

Integrated filing system. You need a place to keep all those tracking forms. The simplest approach is an A-Z index so you can file each form by the name of the associated project or person. One set of A-Z tabs can double as the dividers for the filing system and as the pages of your personal telephone directory.

161

As with any other purchase, you'll need to educate yourself about the range of options, prices and features before you buy. Some products include additional features such as delegation management, meeting management and project planning. Some include training, some make training optional, others have no training available. Make sure the one you get can help you today and can grow with your needs into the future.

MORE TIPS

✦ If you are planning to buy your first system, change to a different brand, or are considering changing to a new size, here's an inexpensive way to experiment. Purchase just the refills, lined paper, and a three-ring binder in the correct size. Try the undated calendar pages for a month or two. When you are sure the system works for you, then invest in the dated pages, a vinyl or leather binder, the specific forms, etc.

✦ Appointments: Some people don't have enough appointments to warrant having a book. For years I have used a legal size clip board with a month-at-a-glance calendar on it. On one end I clip frequently-used phone numbers and cards for beauty shop, etc. I also use it like a tickler file in that when I have directions for an appointment or other papers to keep handy, I put them just behind this month's calendar on the clip board. It is very portable and easy to use by the telephone.

26
READING
MATERIAL

"Reading furnishes the mind only with material for knowledge; it is thinking [that] makes what we read ours."

— John Locke

MAGAZINES, CATALOGS, NEWSPAPERS & BOOKS
Terry Prince

Magazines

If you are like most people, you start to read a magazine and put it down with every good intention of finishing it. Before the time arrives to pick it up again, another equally fascinating issue has arrived. Be realistic about your subscription: if you haven't read the last three issues of a magazine it is time to end your subscription.

Be selective about the magazines you save. Don't save an entire magazine for just one article. If you have decided to save issues of a magazines, invest in magazine holders. They come in a variety of sizes and materials, plastic, paper and even acrylic.

Unfortunately, few recycling programs accept magazines for recycling. If you have magazines in good condition, consider donating them to nursing homes, children's schools, hospitals and clinics, or anywhere individuals have to wait for a period of time. In some areas nonprofit associations hold annual book sales and include magazines for resale.

It's time to change our attitude about magazines. Think of them as a vacation for the mind: experience them, then get rid of them. Remember we do not have to be the librarians of the world. Most libraries are able to supply most popular magazines along with research and reference services.

Suggested Retention for Magazines

People Profiles	2 weeks
News Weeklies	2 weeks
Women's Magazines	1 month
Computer Magazines	2 years
Fashion	3 years
Cooking	5 years
Decorating	5 years
Science	5 years

Catalogs

The easiest way to deal with catalogs is to save only those from which you know you may be ordering. Use a small box and corral them. Get the box out when you feel the urge to go shopping. When the box gets filled, throw out the old issues.

Reducing the number of catalogs sent to your household is possible by writing to:

Direct Marketing Association,
Mail Preference Service
P. O. Box 9008
Farmingdale, NY 11735-9008

Request that your name be removed from their lists. This does not work overnight, but many of my clients have found that they start to see results in about six months.

Newspapers

Set limits on your newspaper holdings. Allow dailies to remain in your house for a maximum of two days, then put them in the recycling bin.

Cut out articles you want to save as you see them or, at the very latest, the end of the day. Otherwise you will forget which issue and have to spend extra time searching through back issues. If scissors are not handy, tear out the page; then fold and stack pages neatly in your reading file.

Suggested Retention for Newspapers	
Daily Papers	2 days
Weekly Papers	1 week

Books

Group your books into three basic classifications: non-fiction, fiction and reference. Consider storing the categories in different rooms or bookcases to make the distinction apparent.

If you don't have space to put your books on display, don't save them. Recycle your books.

- Take them to a used book store for trade or cash.
- Some associations hold annual book sales and need donations.
- Start a book swap with friends that share your taste in books.
- Use the library for your books and let it take care of purchasing and storing them for you.

MORE TIPS

✦ A good place to store current magazines is a pretty basket by your favorite chair. Just make sure you put the newest magazines on the bottom.

✦ Cancel subscriptions to magazines you never have the chance to read.

✦ After looking at a catalog, throw it out if you don't care to order anything. If you decide to place an order, tear or cut out the appropriate page(s), tear off the cover with the portion of the mailing label and pull out the order form. Staple these together and throw out the rest. Once you have placed the order, taken delivery and pronounced yourself satisfied, throw out the papers you saved to keep track of the order. You can be sure you will receive another catalog soon.

✦ Consider using a basket or tote bag with rigid sides to hold reading materials, so that they can be carried with you to appointments or more convenient reading locations. Keep an assortment of tools handy in the basket or tote to use in processing information as you read: scissors (to clip articles), sticky notes and pen/pencil (to write memos for routing), highlighters (to emphasize important points), stapler and/or paper clips (to keep pages of articles together). If you read a lot and regularly save articles, consider using an accordion file to sort articles you clip into appropriate file categories as you read. Use sticky notes to make temporary labels for the categories as you go.

✦ When reading, it is helpful to highlight passages as you go. This helps you when you are reviewing the information later and it is helpful to others reading the material after you (perhaps at your recommendation).

✦ Clip articles, note the source and throw the rest of the periodical away. Don't read an interesting article and then set it aside promising to cut it out later. What that produces is two piles: the original reading pile and another pile containing things you know you need to keep but now have to re-read to remember why you saved the magazine initially.

✦ Be realistic about the amount of information you can read and absorb. Limit the number of subscriptions you take and clip articles as soon as you read them. Throw the rest of the periodical away or recycle it.

From the Lillian Vernon Catalog

168

27

RECYCLING

"What was once routinely thrown into the garbage may not belong there anymore."

— Diann Abbott, City of Palo Alto, CA

THE ECOLOGICAL OFFICE

✦ Use mechanical pencils and refillable pens. Throw-aways are an environmental no-no.

✦ Have two wastebaskets near your desk: one for rubbish, the other for recyclable paper.

✦ Use white paper (easier to recycle) as much as possible and save the colored paper for important flyers.

✦ Pretty new containers or file folders are great for public presentations, but less visible containers can be recycled: e.g., bank check boxes are perfect desk drawer organizers; shoe boxes adequately hold video and audio tapes.

✦ If you can say it on *one* page, by changing type size or editing, you can save paper.

✦ Recycle empty paper towel and toilet paper tubes (covered with contact paper if you wish) and control extra cord length at the same time. Fold the electric cord into "S" curves, making sure that the sections are long enough so that the bends will not be compressed after the cord is stored (a tightly bent electrical wire is potentially dangerous). Now insert the cord into the tube.

✦ Use the blank back of a sheet of printed paper to print drafts of documents (if your memory typewriter or printer will take it safely), or to hand-write drafts. These full-size pages also can be neatly torn into halves or quarters to serve as scratch paper

✦ Keep blank note pad paper in one spot where you will really use it (by the phone or on top of the fridge, for example). Be sure to keep a usable pen or pencil with it.

✦ Know and follow your local recycling rules. Separate paper and other waste as requested, and use suggested methods and materials for containing your refuse securely until the recycle company picks it up. Incidentally—if possible, avoid leaving paper products out in the rain. Your garbage collector's back will appreciate your thoughtfulness.

MORE TIPS

✦ Your dry cleaner may recycle the plastic bags that they place over the clean clothes. Ask!

✦ If your city doesn't accept magazines and catalogs, check the nearby recycling centers. A neighbor or friend may be willing to take turns with you to deliver your collections. This could be the single best thing you can do to reduce waste.

28

SHOPPING

"[The customers] had a tendency to stop shopping when their baskets became too full or heavy."

— Sylvan N. Goldman
On why he designed the first wheeled grocery carts

✦ Don't rely on memory, or fall victim to impulse. Make a shopping list and stick to it. It will not only save you time in the store and ensure that you get what you need, it will also help you avoid impulse purchases, or stocking up on something you already have.

✦ Give consumable gifts. Your friends will thank you for the lack of clutter.

✦ Resist the "gimmes." When considering a purchase, ask yourself if you really want it and have the right space for it, if you are willing to clean and maintain it properly, and if you will still *see* it one week, one month, or one year from now.
My friend Steve had an anti-madness method that he applied to the potential purchase of any item that had not actually been on his shopping list. He walked out of the store, away from the yard sale or past the rental counter and took a walk for ten minutes to an hour, depending on the cost of the goodie. If at the end of his walk the item was still on his mind, he went back and got it. Nine times out of ten he had forgotten all about it. I have tried this and it really works!

171

✦ When shopping for clothes, take color swatches so you don't buy colors that won't blend with mix-and-match outfits. Then ask yourself, "Do I really need another green blouse that looks like the three I already have?" Maybe a scarf would be more useful and less expensive.

✦ Post a list on the refrigerator to make note of things to buy. Let housemates know that if an item is listed there, it will be bought on the next run to the grocery store.

✦ Create individual shopping lists to take with you to the various stores where you usually shop—grocery, health food, discount, office supply.

✦ Put film drop and pick-up on the weekly shopping list. Ditto for dry cleaning.

✦ When you get your film developed, use self-stick return address labels (which include your phone number) on the photo packet the store sends in, and watch the clerk be impressed!

29

STORAGE

"Space and light and order. Those are things that men need just as much as they need bread or a place to sleep."

— Le Corbusier

General Rules

✦   Store infrequently used items high or low or behind other items.

✦   Keep things close to where you use them. This is one of the best ways to stay organized.

✦   Be consistent about where you put things. It makes it easier to remember where they are.

Apartment Living

✦   Use modular systems (cubes, chests, boxes, stackable shelves, carts on wheels). When you move, these items can be reused in new ways and places.

Arts and Crafts

✦   Makeup and hair care organizers, fishing tackle boxes and tool chests are effective containers for organizing art and craft supplies. Your choice would depend on the sizes, variety of sizes and number of compartments needed.

✦   Use roll-on deodorant bottles for poster paint dispensers: remove the ball, rinse the container, fill it with paint and replace the ball. Store the bottle with the top in place.

✦   A pencil bag is a good place to store crochet needles, safety pins, scissors and tape measure. Everything will be at hand when you crochet, and it is a good way to take things along when you travel.

Bathrooms

✦   Install pull-out drawers under the vanity.

Cassette Tapes

✦   Number each tape with a label and marker pen. Write the name of each tape and its number on a 3 X 5 index card and file the tapes alphabetically by title. Store tapes numerically in racks or shelving. To find a tape, look it up by its title in the card box; retrieve it by number in the cassette tape file.

Cleaning Products

✦   Keep oily cloths that you use for cleaning and/or polishing products in separate reclosable plastic bags, secured to the container with a rubber band. (If cloths are not put in plastic bags, the oil will cause the rubber band to disintegrate.)

Instruction Manuals

✦   Store manuals next to the object to which they belong (under the answering machine, on top of the VCR, in the glove compartment, beside the TV or taped to the back). Tape business cards for vendors, dealers and service people to the bottom or side of the corresponding appliance.

✦ Alternatively, you may want to keep all instruction manuals, guarantee cards, parts lists and order forms that come with household equipment and appliances together in a special file (perhaps a stationery box) and give it a permanent and readily accessible home in an office or kitchen drawer.

Linen Closets

✦ Install pull-out drawers on one or two shelves so that small items are easily accessible and manageably contained.

✦ Put sets of towels away together, rather than separating them by size. Put the folded bath towels on the bottom and then the hand towels and washcloths side by side on top of the bath towels.

Makeup Products

✦ Keep those you use everyday in a box or basket rather than separated by kind. Just pull out the basket to put on your makeup, and when finished, drop everything back into the basket and put it away.

Shelves

✦ Shelves above doorways make great extra storage space for oversized or little-used items. They are easy to make with a painted board and brackets and can be screwed into a wooden door frame.

✦ Under-the-shelf hanging racks can be used in any cupboard or closet to contain small items and expand usable space.

Wall or Ceiling Space

✦ Use pegboards to hang objects close at hand, especially in the kitchen, bathroom, office, bedroom, shop or garage.

30
TAXES

"Our constitution is in actual operation; everything appears to promise that it will last; but in this world nothing is certain but death and taxes."

— Benjamin Franklin

TAX TIPS AND AUDIT PROOFING
Carole Kane

How to Keep as Much of Your Income as You Can

Finance charges paid on personal loans and credit cards are no longer deductible. Consolidate credit card debt and switch to equity line mortgage interest, which is still deductible.

If you operate your business in or out of your home, devote one room exclusively to running it and deduct that percentage of your rent, utilities, insurance and cleaning. If you own your home, reduce your self-employment tax by taking that percentage of interest, taxes and depreciation off your business profits.

Increase your auto expenses by using a percentage of your actual expenses and depreciation for your car. This is frequently greater than the standard mileage rate.

179

Hundreds of deductible dollars can be saved by listing clothes and other goods donated to legal charities, and itemizing their value. For example, a jacket is worth $10 to $50, and a suit, $10 to $90.

If someone has not paid to you moneys owed, the amount due may be deductible, with proper substantiation.

In order to deduct meals and entertainment expenses, it is necessary only to write the name of the person, the amount (including the tip) and the business you discussed.

Inheritances are not taxable to you unless you sell afterwards at a profit.

Save all those home improvement receipts! When you sell your home they will reduce taxable profits if you chose not to buy another home, or if you buy a less expensive one.

If you earn money on a hobby deduct the expenses to neutralize the income.

If you get a giant refund each year, change your withholding so you get to use that money during the year. Put it in a money market account and keep the interest yourself.

Frequently Missed Deductions

- DMV fees
- Safe deposit box fees
- Employment-related education
- Books or magazines about investment
- Car washing for an auto used in business
- Job-hunting costs, even if you don't succeed
- Auto mileage for maintaining rental property
- Subscriptions to business journals and trade magazines related to your work.

Best Tax Shelters

- Rental property
- Owning your own home
- SEP retirement plans for the self employed, or IRAs.
  Note: You can use your IRA or SEP money interest-free for 60 days without incurring an IRS penalty.

How to Audit-Proof Your Tax Return

No one is completely immune from a tax audit because some returns are chosen at random by the IRS. However, others are chosen for an audit because they contain items that trigger IRS scrutiny.

Use actual totals of receipts or checks. Rounded figures look like estimates, which are not allowed.

Double check all mathematical calculations on your return. A mistake in addition or subtraction will result in your return getting kicked out of the IRS computer and into the hands of an employee at the IRS. Once this happens, the likelihood of an audit will increase.

Watch out for the "red flags," and have your documentation for these items. A return that shows $80,000 income and $50,000 in deductions will arouse suspicion. However, don't cheat yourself either, just because you are afraid of being audited. Keep the receipts as well as the canceled checks. The IRS wants both.

Attach an explanation to your return for any items that you think the IRS may question.

On the following page is a list of some items that are notorious for attracting special attention from the IRS:

- Overstated interest deductions
- Overstated medical expenses
- Questionable home office deductions
- Inaccurate capital gains and losses
- Overstated travel and entertainment expenses
- Undocumented charitable deductions
- Filing a Schedule C (Anyone who is self-employed should prepare Schedule C carefully, because it's a favorite target of the IRS. Be sure to have back-up records.)
- Using the wrong tax preparer (The IRS keeps a list of tax preparers whom it considers unscrupulous and audits their work more often than average.)

When parents want to transfer real estate to their grown children, taxes can be a problem. If they sell the property to the children, a capital gain may result. If they give an outright gift of a valuable property, they'll be hit with a big gift tax. Use this tax-saving tactic instead: Make annual gifts of a partial interest in the property, each gift being equal in value to the annual gift tax exclusion ($20,000 per recipient when the gift is made by a married couple, $10,000 when made by an individual).

If an IRS agent comes to your door, you do not have to invite the person in. Don't! Contact your tax preparer.

Save your tax returns forever, in case the IRS or the state loses them. You only need to save your receipts, checks and documentation materials for seven years. Save documentation of all real estate and equipment transactions for seven years after you sell an item.

Depreciation is complicated. Be sure you know what you are doing.

ASK YOUR ADVISORS
Tudi Baskay

It is important to check with your tax advisor before purging your tax files. In some cases, you might want to consult your lawyer, investment advisor or real estate broker as well. This list contains questions you might ask so that your records will be as simple as possible without exposing you to undue future risk.

- How many years should I keep copies of my income tax returns?

- What supporting documents must be kept; for how long?

- If I've been audited, how long do I have to keep those records?

- How long should I keep canceled checks and paid bills that do not relate to taxes?

- If I pay by check, do I need to keep the bills for non-tax items?

- What papers pertaining to legal actions must I keep, and for how long?

- What home improvement papers do I need to keep?

- What records of investments and real estate transactions must I keep for tax purposes?

- How long after the sale of property must I keep back-up records?

- Once a disputed bill is settled, how long need I keep that paperwork?

- Do I need to keep expired or canceled insurance policies?

- What records, if any, do I need to keep forever?

TAX GUIDELINES
Tudi Baskay

This is a general guideline for setting up permanent personal income tax records. A tax preparer has checked it for accuracy; nevertheless, you should have your own tax preparer pass judgment on it to ensure that it fits your tax situation correctly.

Both federal and state tax back-up records should be kept for seven years after the due date (April 15th) or the filing date, whichever is later. These records include paid bills, canceled checks, bank statements and any other papers that were used to support your return. After seven years, these documents can be thrown away. Some tax advisors suggest keeping the return itself permanently.

As long as you own a piece of real estate, an investment, or business asset, you should keep records of when you bought it, how much you paid for it, and the date, cost, and nature of any improvements or reinvestments you made. These records should be kept with your tax records for seven years after the sale of an asset. After real estate has been sold, you need to keep the signed settlement papers in your permanent files. All other papers can be discarded without tax consequences.

Non-tax-related checks should be kept for three years. It may be easier, if space allows, to store them with your permanent tax files and purge them at the seven-year mark.

MORE TIPS

✦ Set up files with tax-related documents accumulated together during the year, so you don't have to sort and retrieve them on April 14th.

✦ Donate unwanted items for a tax deduction. Itemize the list and save the receipt you obtain when you donate them to a nonprofit organization.

✦ If you routinely deposit receipts into more than one type of cash account (savings, checking, CDs, mutual funds, stocks, partnerships), photocopy the checks and deposit slips and file them together by account number and financial institution. This may prove very helpful later should you need to reconstruct a sequence of transactions.

✦ It's a good idea to start a new check register on January 1 of each year for each account. Be careful not to label it automatically with the number of the year that just ended!

31
TELEPHONES

"...the telephone shone as brightly as a weapon kept polished by daily use."

— Colette

VOICE MAIL AND
ANSWERING MACHINE ETIQUETTE

When leaving your name and phone number on an answering machine, *slow down* or *repeat* the information. People have a tendency to speed up with numbers they know very well, making it difficult for the receiver to jot it down.

When leaving a message on a machine, be specific about the reason for your call and the best times to return your call. Phone tag and time wasted are minimized if a simple question or answer is left on the machine.

Respect the privacy needs of the person you are calling. If you are not sure whether a third party (a roommate or co-worker, for example) might find himself listening to the message you left, consider omitting anything that might be embarrassing or hurtful to the person you are calling or the third party, were someone else to hear it.

Some things are just inappropriate to be left on a machine. That the person being called is being fired, or notification of a death, deserve to be handled by two live human beings speaking with each other, if at all possible. In such a case expedience *must* take a back seat to thoughtfulness and kindness.

MORE TIPS

✦ Place the telephone on your non-dominant side so that holding the phone leaves your dominant hand free to make notes. Better yet, invest in a headset so you can have both hands free and keep your neck and shoulders from becoming tense.

✦ Design a phone interview sheet for gathering information from potential clients who call you. List name, address, home and work phone numbers, along with some pertinent questions to ask to help you evaluate their needs. This is a great prompt when you get an unexpected call and your mind is somewhere else.

✦ Avoid idle hands while on the telephone. Wash dishes, clean out a drawer, fold clothes, etc. In your office, pick out a routine task or two (such as updating your address file) that you can work on when you are put on "hold." It's a good way to lower your frustration level and increase your efficiency.

✦ Minimize others' call-waiting irritation by assuring the original caller that you will be only a few seconds, and then firmly inform the other caller immediately, even if she is calling long distance, that you are on the other line. *Get back to caller number one ASAP*. Leaving someone hanging on "hold" is insulting and rude, no matter who they are or what your reason.

✦ Consider alternatives to call waiting. A second line that connects to an answering service, voice mail or an answering machine are some possibilities. Depending on your budget and what is available in your area, you may be able to set up one or more additional lines in such a way that your conversation is not disturbed *and* an overflow caller is able to leave a message, rather than having to interrupt you or contend with a busy signal.

At this writing, some phone companies offer this type of no frills voice mail service for $6 per month. One company offers the following features at the base rate: an outgoing message (OGM) in your own voice; five incoming lines; the ability to play part or all of a message, save a message unheard or save a previous message as a new incoming message; fast rewind, fast forward and pause (for taking notes); an alternate OGM tailored to a special situation (e.g. "Diana, I'm in transit so you can't reach me, but I'll meet you at the box office at 7:15."), which flips back to the regular OGM when the alternate one is no longer needed. And all of the above are accessible by remote from any phone number.

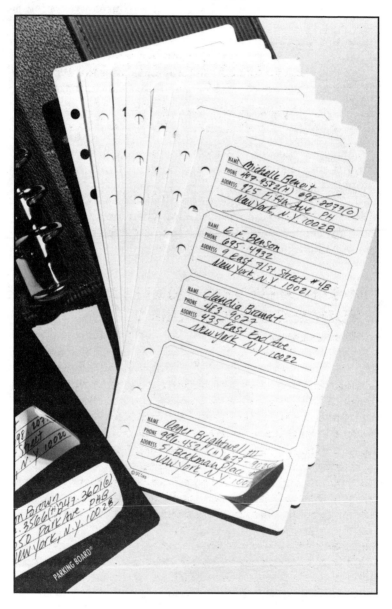

190

32

TELEPHONE & ADDRESS BOOKS

"Let the telephone help you share the gifts you've got."

— Teri Fockler, Pacific Bell

TIPS FOR EFFECTIVE TELEPHONE & ADDRESS DIRECTORIES
Lee Victoria Larsen

Getting organized has its challenges. Recently, one of my clients called me to report with exasperation, "Okay, now I've started to write everything down but my desktop is more awash in paper clutter than ever before! What now?" I did my best to reassure him that the write-it-down habit was the first step out of crisis management into time management. After doing an initial paper sort, he was surprised that more than 50% of his papers contained information needed in his telephone and address directory. The rest were assigned to action files.

It is amazing how many of those various papers and notes that lurk in our offices are there because of a name or phone number that we don't want to lose track of. This fact makes the directory a key system to have up and running.

Here are some suggestions for keeping up to date with your directory data:

• Set up a desktop action file labeled Update Directory, or use a box, basket or drawer that can accommodate a range of paper sizes. Begin now to consistently put all new information into this designated place. This way, you will always know where to find a name or number: either in your directory or in your designated holding place.

• Integrate only that business card data into your directory which you will actually use. Shamelessly throw away all other business cards. Avoid using those plastic business card holders at all costs! In the meantime, use an interim storage file, box, basket or drawer, and then easily incorporate these into your system when you update. In some cases, the card can be attached directly to a rotating file card.

• Select a system for your directory that makes sense with your work situation and personal management style. Rotary or file-box style systems are most prevalent because it is possible to maintain alphabetization easily while adding and deleting, and because they are neat (no crossed out entries on a page, just discard the old card, fill out a new card and re-file it).

Loose leaf binder-style appointment book directories have their virtues, too: if it is a portable size and you are conscientious about carrying it with you, it will provide you with all you need when you need it, wherever you may be. Another type of book that can work well is the pocket-size variety. This is a good solution if your appointment book is bulky or not often needed outside of the office.

• Divide all names and numbers into "white pages" and "yellow pages." This is simpler than it sounds: Imagine moving out of state. All schools, doctors, repair professionals and stores would change. These resources, which typically are filed by category, comprise your yellow pages. Your friends and family with whom you always want to stay in touch would stay with you. Because they are typically filed alphabetically by name, they are your white pages.

• Be creative. Take license to set up your directory so it uniquely suits you. First ask, "Is this listing for the white or yellow pages?" If it's a yellow page listing, then ask yourself, "Where will it make sense to me to look for this information?" Then decide whether to list alphabetically, by subject, a blend of both or to cross reference at the outset just to ensure the smoothest start. If you have a large number of listings and if you do choose to cross reference, I recommend indicating so with an "x" or an asterisk. This keeps later editing simple.

Barbara Hemphill in her book *Taming the Paper Tiger* says, *"There is no law which says that a rotary phone-file card can be used only for addresses and phone numbers. The file is a perfect place to record bits of information. . ., such as the social security numbers for your family or the combination to your child's bike lock. . . . Think of the file as a mini-file for odd bits of information."*

Everyone has experienced the panic at one time or another of being unable to find a phone number or address when it was needed. Surely having a directory at your fingertips which consistently provides the needed information is an invaluable asset. Realizing the role an up-to-date directory plays in the daily challenge of conquering paper clutter adds new incentive to consistently tend to our directories!

BUILD FLEXIBILITY INTO
YOUR ADDRESS BOOKS
Terry Prince

When creating a new address book, plan on the project taking two weeks to complete. Break the alphabet up into nine letter groups (A-C, D-F, G-I, J-L, M-O, P-R, S-U, V-X, Y-Z). Enter the names and addresses into one group each day. This will enable you to take your time and avoid sloppy handwriting and transposed numbers. If you have many relatives with the same last name or a very large number of contacts in a particular letter of the alphabet, plan one day to write that letter in, and leave the other letters of its group until the following day.

For maximum flexibility, write the names in ink, but use pencil for addresses and phone numbers. This makes it easy to change information for those who move often.

Use only address books you can add pages to.

It's a good idea to have one master address book which never leaves your house. Write all address changes in this book first. Cultivate the habit of making changes in your master address book as soon as you receive them.

MORE TIPS

✦   Businesses or individuals whom you contact for categorical purposes need not have a card for a single address/phone number or a single business card. Create a generic category card and keep the information there. On one card, or in one section of your address directory, identify the categories, so you'll have a handy reference if you forget what some of them are. You can also create cards for such things as items loaned and important information like your driver's license number, social security number, employer's and landlord's phone numbers.

✦ In addition to alphabetical dividers, buy blank dividers that you can insert behind the alphabetical dividers in loose leaf books or rotary card files. This is your resource section. Your resource section is for people that you may some day need to contact or that you can refer to others. Assign a different occupation or definition to each divider. For example: accountants, attorneys, banks, computers, engineers, florists, interior designers, insurance agents, marketing, meeting rooms, office supplies, organizers, printers, real estate agents, travel agencies, training & development. Attach business cards to or write the necessary information on the appropriate pages or rolling file cards and file them under the proper category.

✦ For individuals who are important to you as clients or friends, make notes on their cards with pertinent information like their family members' names (including pets) , when and where you met, and their product preferences. Record directions to the person's home or office on the back of his card or in a separate Directions file, to avoid repeated requests for the same information.

✦ If you carry a planning notebook with loose leaf pages, computerize the names, addresses and telephone numbers you usually carry with you. This allows you to update them and eliminates the necessity of rewriting them each year when you get a new calendar.

✦ Don't overlook telephone directory computer software. Most programs let you print out pages in a variety of sizes and sort data in a number of different ways (by zip code or categories, for example). These electronic tools make computer directories easy to update. Imagine never having to redo your entire address book again!

✦ Never use the annual phone book cover to write your household numbers in. Take a sheet of paper and write all your frequently called numbers. Then make copies of this list for your office and other household telephones. Cover the lists with sheet protectors to prevent them from being used as message pads. Update the list as required. Place or post your lists near your busiest or central household telephone.

✦ If you never seem to get around to putting new names in your rotary directory or address books, dump business cards, scraps of envelopes with name and phone numbers (likewise scraps of napkins, paper bags, or deposit slips) into a file labeled Addresses. It won't be fancy or pretty, but at least it will keep all your information in one place!

✦ Leave your primary directory at home and/or in your office. Carry a second directory with you that contains the numbers you are likely to need in the field. In the event that it is lost or stolen, you can easily replace it.

✦ Insist that each member of your family carry a short list of emergency numbers in their wallet or purse, school bag or backpack. If you live in earthquake country, this list should include at least one out-of-state contact number.

33

TICKLER FILES

"Abruptly the poker of memory stirs the ashes of recollection and uncovers a forgotten ember, still smoldering down there, still hot, still glowing, still red as red."

— William Manchester
from *Good-bye Darkness: A Memoire of the Pacific War*

HOW TO SET UP TICKLER FILES
Barbara Raleigh

A tickler file is a system of managing information by date or time. Within any individual section of the tickler file system you will have a variety of information to deal with: bills to pay, letters to answer, phone calls to return, decisions to make (such as, do you want to sign up for a seminar or summer activities for the kids.).

One great thing about a tickler system is that if you find that you can't do everything in today's file, you can transfer the leftover tasks to the next day or week simply by placing those items in the appropriate files.

Tickler files can be made using many different kinds of materials. The two most common tickler file systems use hanging file folders and index cards, respectively. A hanging folder system holds more information and larger pieces of correspondence, so it is the best choice if you regularly process large volumes of information. Index card files are very useful for tracking sales calls and client/prospect contacts.

Setting up Your System

Using either an index card box with dividers or a set of hanging files, make a divider or file for each month of the year (January through December) and a divider or file for each day of the month (1 to 31). The remaining directions will refer to index cards, but the method is the same when using hanging folders.

Complete a separate card for each item you need to remember or follow up on. For example, if the system is designed to track client contacts, write a person's name, telephone number, and why you need to call. Put the follow-up date, in pencil, in the upper right corner.

If the follow-up is to be made in the current month, file the card behind the divider for the date you will make the call. For example, if it is June 10th, and you need to follow up on June 25th, file the card behind the number 25 divider or in the number 25 folder.

If a follow-up is to be made in a future month, file the card behind the appropriate monthly divider. For example, if it is June 10th and you need to follow up on July 10th, file the card behind the July divider.

Each day of the current month you will pull the cards for that day and make your follow-up calls. As each call is made, note any pertinent information about the conversation on the card, and if another follow-up is needed, note the new date of the next contact in the corner of the card. Re-file the card in the next appropriate day or month. On the last day of each month, take all the cards from behind the name of the next month and sort them into specific date sections as above.

PUTTING IT ALL TOGETHER: TICKLER SYSTEMS, ACTION FILES & CALENDARS

Arleen Westcott

A traditional 43-file tickler system (a file for each month and a file for each day of the month, 1 to 31) may seem too much for you. It is for some people. Here are some other options that may work better for you.

Try a tickler system with one file labeled for each month and either five weekly files (labeled First Week, Second Week, etc.), or two bi-weekly files (one labeled 1-15 and one labeled 16-31). Place the weekly or the bi-monthly files behind the current month's labeled folder and reposition each file as time passes.

Another way of managing mail and information is with an action file system. An action file system is set up by labeling files with the frequent actions that need to be taken (read, decide, pay, mail, etc.) When opening mail, decide on the first action that needs to be taken with each piece of information and place the item in the appropriate labeled file. This system uses action rather than due date as the primary sorting criteria, and is useful in grouping activities when planning your days.

If you like the idea of action files, but you also want or need time-related files, the two systems can be combined quite effectively. For example, you can divide an action file called To Pay into two files labeled 1-15 and 16-31.

No matter which system you choose for managing information, none will work unless you refer to it regularly. A calendar system can help you make your plans. Following are effective ways to combine your paper system with a calendar:

A monthly calendar on the wall or desktop to refer to makes it easy to see the month when deciding where to file information in the tickler system. You will also find a month-at-a-glance and/or weekly desk calendar very valuable in planning your time so that everything in your tickler file gets done on time, instead of piling up until you become overwhelmed. (See also chapters on Planning, Planning Notebooks and Time.) Here's how to use a calendar in conjunction with tickler and action files:

When you set up your action files ask yourself "What is a realistic amount of time for me to spend on this activity every week?" You may decide you need only 10 minutes twice a week, or 15 minutes once a week, or perhaps you need more. Schedule yourself for six weeks out. If you are using a dated tickler system for contact follow-up, check each date for the month and note how many calls need to be made. Then estimate the amount of time required to complete the calls. Whatever you decide, then mark in your calendar those dates and times, as if they are appointments—because they are!

The key to using a calendar successfully is to make appointments with yourself easy to keep. Begin with shorter periods of time rather than longer, and gradually increase your stamina for various kinds of tasks.

Make your plan easy for yourself, and you will be successful in maintaining your paper management system. More importantly, you will be in control of the comings and goings in your life, with less stress and greater peace of mind.

34
TIME

"Hurry is a fundamental error."

— Chinese Proverb

FIND EXTRA TIME IN YOUR DAY: LEARN TO USE YOUR TIME MORE CONSCIOUSLY

Diana Dring

I wish I had a dollar for every time I've heard someone say "I'd like to get organized, but I can't find the time." The truth is, no one ever really "finds" time for anything, we make time for those things that are truly important to us. Most of us waste more time on unimportant activities each day than we realize. Simply by becoming more aware of our time-use habits and consciously changing our behavior one day at a time, we can significantly increase both the amount of time we have available and the amount of satisfaction we experience from the things we do accomplish. Here are seven suggestions that can really make a difference:

1. Focus on your priorities and goals. To use time well, we must be aware of our priorities and goals and concentrate on activities that support them. Most wasted time results from becoming sidetracked: saying yes to activities that seem urgent but don't really contribute to our personal mission. The phone rings and we answer it *automatically*. We say yes to the request of the caller, again *automatically*. We change our direction in response to whatever may be happening in our thoughts, emotions or environment at the moment. And at the end of the day, we wonder where the time went.

In addition, each of us fulfills personal, family, career, community and social roles and has priorities in each area. When we regularly neglect one or more of our roles, our quality of life inevitably suffers. Procrastination is a type of compulsive wasting of time that often results from lack of balance in our activities. For example, when we neglect to schedule enough recreation time, we may procrastinate as a way of stealing time to relax. Unfortunately, the result of procrastination is rarely relaxation, but usually increased worry and self-criticism, which only exacerbates the problem. So it's also important to attend to our priorities and work towards goals consistently in a balanced way.

To set balanced goals, first identify your most important priorities in each of the areas mentioned above. Next, identify one or more specific goals you want to accomplish in each priority area. Then list the first two actions you need to take to begin moving forward toward each goal. Make taking these steps the core of your schedule for the coming week. Make appointments with yourself to complete the task you identified for each of your goals.

2. Plan your schedule a week in advance. It's been said that every minute you spend planning how to use your time can save you up to four minutes in carrying out your plan. Practically speaking, that means that 15 minutes per day could save you up to an hour; 30 minutes could save you two hours. An hour a week could save you half a day!

Plans save time because they keep us conscious of how we *choose* to use our time. They help us stay focused on what is most important and let go of what is not, recognize distractions and decline to be diverted. Conversely, if we determine that an interruption *does* require our attention, a well-conceived plan lets us rearrange priorities without sacrificing anything of real importance.

Planning your schedule for an entire week at a time allows you to see time from a broader perspective than simply day-to-day. A weekly plan allows you to see the relationships between blocks of time and what needs to be done. It allows you greater flexibility when activities must be shifted around to accommodate unexpected events. It helps you maintain a more realistic perspective on the amount of time available to accomplish tasks and projects.

3. Balance short-range and long-range activities. Spending too much time focusing on the immediate (looming deadlines, crises and other urgent matters) can overwhelm us with feelings of constant pressure, for which, in turn, we may tend to compensate by escaping into empty, trivial activities. The more we regularly attend to longer-range projects and non-urgent tasks, the less often emergencies will occur, and the more discretionary time we will have available.

4. Know how long things take to do. Most people underestimate by a factor of two to four how much time a given activity will require. Not allowing enough time to complete a task comfortably causes us to take on more than we can realistically handle and pack our schedules too tightly. This increases stress and can lead to burnout.

Effective time managers routinely double, triple or quadruple their time estimates for certain activities. Alleviating stress this way allows one to concentrate more fully on the task at hand. Improved concentration can actually speed up completion of the task, leaving extra time to spend on something else.

5. Understand your own energy cycles. Daily fluctuations in physical energy significantly affect our productivity. Identify your energy peaks and valleys. Schedule critical activities when your energy is high or on the way up, and less critical ones when it's ebbing.

6.   Be aware of your counter-productive habits. Spend a week keeping close track of how you spend your time. Note when you are distracted by interruptions and what kinds of things are hardest to say no to. Monitor how much time different activities take to do. Pay attention to when and why you change your mind or your direction. Especially watch for things you do habitually without thinking and notice how they affect your progress through the week.

More than anything else, optimizing our time is a function of how conscious we are of the way we function in time. The more aware we are, the more choice, control and breathing room we have.

7.   Ask for help when you need it. Sometimes even the most well-intentioned scheduling doesn't keep you on track or on time. When this happens, it's useful to seek outside assistance for a detached perspective on issues that you may have trouble seeing objectively yourself. A professional organization coach can help you break through overwhelm, procrastination and paralysis and get moving again. We offer completely non-judgmental support through the process of change. Our goal is to help you master your environment and schedule, so time becomes a valuable tool instead of a slave driver.

CONQUERING PROCRASTINATION
Odette Pollar

Do you wait until Christmas Eve to do the bulk of your Christmas shopping? When filing your taxes, do you wait until April 12th to start sorting through the shoe boxes filled with receipts? And then do you wait in those long lines at the post office to mail the return? When a member of your organization has a complaint that you need to address, do you find other items suddenly become more pressing? If so, you are not alone.

Procrastination is the continual avoidance of starting or seeing a task through to completion. It is one of the most common stumbling blocks to managing time. Straightening the desk, reading the mail, cleaning the house, washing the car, et al., are all tasks that have to be done. But if, by doing any of those tasks, you avoid the A-number-one top priorities, like filing your taxes, making follow-up phone calls, implementing a new marketing program or tackling a complicated project, you are procrastinating.

To combat the tendency to put things off start by looking at the underlying causes of delay.

1. Inability to say no. How often have you said yes to demands on your time before evaluating your desire or ability to fulfill them? When you over-commit yourself you can be forced to delay because you are, in fact, unable to find the time. It is often difficult to say no to a request, particularly if the person asking is in need.

2. Fear. The root cause of most avoidance is fear—and there are many kinds: fear of failure, success, rejection, anger, embarrassment or any negative emotion. If you are asked to make a speech, and the thought of standing before an audience is terrifying, what happens? Do you wonder what is going on in the minds of the audience? Do you worry that they will not like, approve of or agree with what you have to say? What if someone asks a question that you cannot answer? This process of anticipation and worry about a worst-case scenario can escalate fear until it becomes unmanageable.

3. An unpleasant task. Very few of us are eager to do something that is distasteful. The longer one avoids it, the more seeming freedom and control one has. The longer one waits, the better the chance the task will go away or someone else will do it. As soon as you procrastinate you get an immediate reward—in this case, not having to start the unpleasant task.

Breaking Through Procrastination

The next time that you are asked to accept yet another thing to do, resist the tendency to answer immediately. Offer to call back the person making the request after you have thought about it. Consider what chairing the fund raising committee really means. Look at your calendar, brush off your resolutions, and most important, determine the true nature of the task. How much of your time, energy and resources will it really take?

When a task is unpleasant, evaluate the need to do it at all. Ask if it can be done less often or more quickly. Is it a task that can be bartered away or hired out? If you must handle it, try to do it sooner rather than later. The longer you wait, the more hateful it becomes. You can spend a great deal of anxious psychic energy doing the job in your mind over and over again. Spend that energy actually doing the task so you can reap the benefits of having it finished.

Do not let fear immobilize you. A good technique to use in lessening its impact is to actively visualize yourself facing and overcoming it. Do you believe that the audience will laugh at you? That they will ask you questions you cannot answer? That they will doubt your expertise? Practice the speech before a mirror, into a tape recorder, before friends. Anticipate the difficult questions and find the answers. Have yourself introduced as an authority in the field with x-number of years experience (if it is true, of course). Ask associates to share tips on how they handle fear and nervousness. Channel that fear into actions to overcome the fear.

When you find yourself procrastinating ask yourself: "What is really so bad about it?" Remember, anticipation is much worse than the actual occurrence can ever be. When you simply are not in the mood to tackle the project, remember: once you start something related to the project, no matter how small that portion may be, you are no longer procrastinating.

CRITERIA FOR PRIORITIZING
Anacaria Myrrha

Important and Urgent. These are tasks that should get first priority.

Important, Not Urgent. These can be scheduled with a little more flexibility. Be sure to give them priority, however, because if you don't, they will become urgent, and you may feel pressured against a deadline.

Urgent, Not Important. Watch out for these! They are often generated from outside sources and can absorb your time like a sponge. They often need not be done at all. Learn to recognize and eliminate them.

Necessary Busywork. These are tasks like house or office maintenance or routine paperwork. They must be done to keep order and harmony, but should not be scheduled during "prime" time. Try doing them as a bridge between difficult tasks, or at the time of your lowest mental acuity.

A Waste of Time. These are tasks that have nothing to do with what is important to you. Ruthlessly eliminate them and use the time to do something you love. You may be amazed and delighted at how much time you gain.

207

HOW TO MAKE A TO DO LIST WORK FOR YOU

Tudi Baskay

A To Do list structures *one* day's activities to ensure that important, time-sensitive tasks are accomplished. It allows you to allot appropriate amounts of time to the most important tasks, and serves as a memory aid. Keep the following things in mind when creating your own lists:

- Limit your list to ten items or fewer. No more than three should take over an hour each to complete.

- Distinguish between what you can control and what you can not. For example, if "appointment with John" is on your list and he reschedules, check that item off the list. You have taken care of it for today!

- Never keep a To Do list for more than 24 hours. Anything important that doesn't get done can be put at the top of tomorrow's list. Let ephemeral items go.

- Include at least one task you will enjoy. Going to a movie is as much something to do as balancing your checkbook.

- Distinguish between *pressing* things and *important* things. Turning in a report on time is pressing; going for a walk with a friend is important. Put both on your list.

- The 80/20 Rule states that, in a list of ten items, 20% of them (two) will produce 80% of the satisfaction value of the entire list. Learn to identify the two and focus your energy on them.

- If something on your list cannot be finished in one day, the item should read, "Work on (Project X) for (amount of time)."

- To Do lists are not for everyone. If you have trouble keeping one, apply these guidelines to a weekly list of no more than 25 items, and see if that solves the problem. Another approach is a Monthly Goal Sheet. A friend of mine puts sticky notes on her calendar and peels them off as each task is completed. Use a system that works for you!

MORE TIPS

✦ When priorities are a problem, ask yourself: "Five years from now, will it really matter?"

✦ Don't try to solve a timing problem all at once. Rome wasn't built in a day. It took time for the problem to reach unmanageable proportions, and it will take time to solve it.

Work in manageable time increments without outside distractions (especially if you are working alone). One- to two-hour sessions are reasonable.

✦ Use a 6 X 9-inch clipboard (larger, if you prefer) with a pen holder attached for on-the-go To Do lists and for jotting down quick notes and thoughts.

✦ Write everything down as a firm commitment. Don't trust your memory. Writing things down enables you to see commitments in relation to one another.

✦ Write everything in your calendar in pencil.

✦ Stay in action. If you get stopped in one area, leave it be for awhile and do something else, before coming back to it.

✦ Have a monthly calendar, as well as a daily or weekly one, in order to see your appointments, project due dates, and other time commitments in a broader perspective.

✦ A rotating annual calendar, viewable month by month, is an excellent place to keep track of those special days that come around yearly, like birthdays and anniversaries. The days of the week are irrelevant since those will change from year to year. You can use an extra month-at-a-glance calendar, and just keep recycling it; or you can buy a pretty notebook made just for this purpose (dates listed, but no day names).

Glance ahead periodically and determine how long it will take your greeting to reach the party. Figure backwards and make note in your current datebook of the date you must mail the card. If you will need to do other things in connection with this (make and wrap a present, for example), you may want to figure your due date and specifically schedule time for this as well.

People I know are always impressed that I "remembered" their special day. The truth is, I remember my mother's birthday and my own. The rest is Organizer Magic, as described above!

✦ Learn to say no! You can't make everyone like you. Learn the difference between friendship and acquaintance.

✦ To avoid interruptions even when your office door is closed, hang a sign on the outside that says Interview in Progress.

✦ To avoid interruptions if you work in an open cubicle, post a sign on the outside panel that says Door Closed.

✦ Don't labor over decisions when sorting things. If you don't know what to do with something, sort it into an "I don't know" category and move on.

✦ An effective way to create more time is to schedule an "hour of power" every weekday in your appointment book. During this time, accept no phone calls or interruptions and focus solely on your top priority project. It works like magic on the rest of your time because a definite momentum builds with your project's success.

✦ It's okay to do something "well enough." Never mind perfect, just do it. My friend's mother suggests doing "a rough job"—just enough to get by for now. "Make do," she says, "you'll live." So far, she's been right.

✦ Centralize your appointments and deadlines in one book and take it everywhere you go. Use that book as headquarters for your life. For example, keep in it your stamps; dry cleaning, shoe repair and photo receipts; checks to be deposited— whatever you need to have with you when you're out and about. Be sure your name and phone number are clearly visible. Don't lose the book!

✦ Schedule time for relaxing, dates with your spouse, events that make you feel fulfilled, time to be alone. This is one way to ensure they will happen instead of being postponed as low priority.

✦ Make sure you schedule time on your calendar for office maintenance. Take time, at least weekly, to straighten up your office and keep things organized.

✦ The "dirty dozen" of time robbers are: perfectionism, procrastination, telephone interruptions, misplaced items, poor organization, failure to set priorities, failure to delegate appropriately, waiting for people, lack of planning, not setting time limits on activities, the inability to say no and drop-in guests.

From the Lillian Vernon Catalog

35

TRAVEL

"The voyage of discovery lies not in finding new landscapes, but in having new eyes."
— Marcel Proust

TRAVEL SMART
Joy Bayshore

Things to Think About Before a Trip:

Airline ticket, itinerary, frequent-flyer identification card, and any coupons for shuttle service. File these together under Travel. If you have a lot of information, consider sub-dividing your travel file for separate air carriers, etc.

A week or two in advance of a trip, make a list of clothes to take. This leaves time for dry cleaning, laundering or mending, and gives you time to revise your wardrobe.

Your carry-on bag should contain at a minimum: cosmetics and toiletries in a travel pouch, one change of socks and underwear, prescription medicines, jewelry or other valuables and snacks such as trail mix, crackers and dried fruit. With these supplies, if you are stuck overnight somewhere, or your luggage is delayed, you are prepared for a minimum of suffering.

As you go down the aisle toward your seat on the airplane, grab a pillow, blanket and magazines from the overhead bins. If you wait for flight attendants to get these items for you, you may miss out.

Travel light. Remove all non-essential papers and other items from your purse and wallet. Use sample sizes of toiletries. Take medications and supplements out of their original bottles and put them in a pill box with labels over the compartments that tell the name and dosage. Remove extra keys from your key ring.

Keep shoe mitts, plastic bags, dress bag and any travel articles stored in suitcases between uses. This saves storage space and you know where to find them.

TRAVEL EASY
Marsha Freid

Put nice clothes on hangers in large plastic bags and fold them in half on top in your suitcase. At your destination, take them out immediately and hang them up. These outfits stay remarkably unwrinkled.

If you travel frequently, use a packing list that stays in a drawer with travel-related items, to remind you of things to take.

For ease in travel, use luggage and carry-ons with wheels. Why schlep a shoulder bag if you don't have to? Select one with expansion capability and removable wheels so that you can check it through baggage handling if necessary.

Pack a flat, soft bag to separate dirty laundry at the end of your trip. Allow extra space in your luggage for gifts and souvenirs. Check the soft luggage with other bags.

Create a list of names and addresses on a computer program that generates labels. Take one or more sheets of labels on your trip to use in addressing postcards.

MORE TIPS

✦ Keep a separate makeup and toiletries bag packed for each member of the family. Use good quality bags and containers with tight-fitting lids. Replenish the kits after each use. To the side of each bag, tape a list of essential additional items such as eye glasses, jewelry, hair accessories and a travel alarm clock. Consult this list when packing.

✦ If you frequently travel to the same place, such as a hometown, former residence, relatives' homes or corporate headquarters, keep a separate folder for each location, which contains local names and phone numbers, maps, restaurants, shopping and sightseeing guides, as well as notations of things to take or do on your next visit there.

III

RECOMMENDED READING

The following print and electronic resources have been recommended by our members as good sources of ideas and information.

Bender, Sue. *Plain and Simple.* San Francisco: Harper and Row, 1989. Explains what it can feel like to be a 90's woman: scattered, disorganized and hungry for order.

Bliss, Edwin G. *Getting Things Done.* New York: Scribner, 1976.

Bolen, Jean Shinoda, M.D. *Goddesses in Every Woman, A New Psychology of Women.* San Francisco: Harper and Row, 1984, pp. 107-131. Explains that bringing order into one's life and home is a deeply felt spiritual need in some women.

Culp, Stephanie. *Conquering the Paper Pile-Up.* Cincinnati: Writer's Digest Books, 1990.

———. *How to Get Organized When You Don't Have the Time.* Cincinnati: Writer's Digest Books, 1986.

Diamond, Susan. *Records Management.* American Management Association, 1991.

Eisenberg, Ronni. *Organize Yourself!* New York: Collier Books, Macmillan, 1986.

Feder, Michal. *Money Minder—A Simple System for Personal Records Management.* Blue Ridge Summit, PA: Tab Books, Liberty House, 1989.

Felton, Sandra. *Messie No More.* Grand Rapids, MI: Baker Book House Company, 1989. The issue of "letting go" is a problem for many people trying to get organized.

Fiore, Neil. *"Stop Wasting Your Time"* and *"Quality Work, Guilt-Free Play"* audio cassette tapes. Audio Renaissance Tapes, Inc., 1988.

Fulton, Alice and **Pauline Hatch.** *It's Here...Somewhere!* Cincinnati: Writer's Digest Books, 1991. Learn how to deal...once and for all...with chronic clutter, lack of space, and the irritating lost-and-found pattern in your home.

Hedrick, Lucy H. *Five Days to an Organized Life.* New York: Dell, 1990. The fast, easy and permanent system for getting things done...and doing things better.

Hemphill, Barbara. *Taming the Paper Tiger.* Washington, D.C.: Kiplinger Books, 1992. Basic user-friendly information on managing paper in your home—what to keep and how to find it when you need it.

Hunt, Diana, Ph.D. and **Pam Hait.** *The Tao of Time.* New York: Fireside Books, Simon & Schuster, 1991. Time management for the real world—a right brain approach that gives you the control you need and the freedom you want.

Jenkins, Colleen. *The Home Owner's Journal.* St. Paul, MN: Blue Sky Marketing, 1990.

Lehmkuhl, Dorothy and **Dolores Cotter Lamping.** *Organizing for the Creative Person.* New York: Crown Trade Paperbacks, 1993. Right-brain styles for conquering clutter, mastering time and reaching your goals.

Mandino, Og. *The Greatest Salesman in the World.* New York: Frederick Fell, 1981.

Myrrha, Anacaria. *Systems By Design, The Practical Art of Personal Organization.* San Rafael, CA: Simple Systems, 1989. A workbook and manual to help you manage your information, energy and paperwork.

Naisbitt, John. *Megatrends for Women.* New York: Villard, 1992. This book is not just for women! It is very inspiring and offers a lot of ideas about starting up a new business and trends to watch.

Pollar, Odette. *Organizing Your Workspace: A Guide to Personal Productivity.* Los Altos, CA: Crisp Publications, Inc., 1992. Using exercises, checklists and easy-to-follow illustrations, this book will help you get and stay organized.

Rossbach, Sarah. *Interior Design with Feng Shui.* New York: E.P. Dutton, 1987.

Schlenger, Sonny. *How to be Organized in Spite of Yourself.* New York: Penguin Group, 1989.

Williamson, Marianne. *Inspired Success.* Los Angeles: Miracle Projects.

———. *Making A Living.* Los Angeles: Miracle Projects.

———. *Work Relationships.* Los Angeles: Miracle Projects.

———. *Success in the World.* Los Angeles: Miracle Projects.

219

Winston, Stephanie. *Getting Organized.* Toronto: George J. McLeod Limited, 1978. The basics of good organizing from nuts-and-bolts how-tos to new ways of thinking about time and the physical environment.

IV

DIRECTORY
OF
MEMBERS

San Francisco
Bay Area Chapter

of the

National
Association of
Professional Organizers
(NAPO)

DIRECTORY OF MEMBERS

- Contributor to this book
- + Golden Circle Member (in business 5 years or more and a NAPO member for at least 1 year)

ABBOTT, EVE
Organizer Extraordinaire
1060 Solano Avenue, Suite 716
Albany, CA 94706
510-528-4950 FAX 510-528-4950

• Accomplish more, in less time, while minimizing stress through personal organization assistance. Streamline your business; increase your profit margin. Create clutter-free environments, control incoming paper, optimize your office and home with solutions that work for you. Orchestrate and enjoy very special occasions. Call Extraordinaire for a complimentary consultation!

ALBRECHT, NANCY
Getting It Together
6541 Snake Road
Oakland, CA 94611
510-773-4640

Simplifying one's life through time and paper management. Or, bringing order and efficiency to the disorganized individual due to paper backlog and clutter. The net result being a place for everything...and everything in its place. The number one reason for being organized is the reduction of stress derived from being organized.

ALBRECHT, SUSIE
2280 Green Street, #203
San Francisco, CA 94123-4753
415-775-6659 FAX 510-867-0628

ALLEN, RICK
Next Actions
18-1/2 Vale Road
Brookfield, CT 06804-3964
203-775-6565 FAX 203-775-6565

+   Executive Coach. Assist managers, entrepreneurs and
executives in implementing significant changes in how they
manage themselves and their business.

ANDERSON, MARY G.
Organizational Consultant
950 Aura Way
Los Altos, CA 94024-5607
415-960-3772 FAX 415-949-1433

• +   Provide one-on-one assistance to busy professionals by
organizing their work through better delegation skills, filing
systems and improved paper flow, and their home life by helping to hire household help and creating a personalized "Home
Management Guide" to assist with keeping order and records
under control.

AURICH, ALAN
Mind Over Matter
236 West Portal Avenue, Suite 455
San Francisco, CA 94127
415-661-3405

Mind Over Matter organizes businesses to be efficient
and effective. Organization is essential for a business to achieve
maximum productivity and increase profitability. Our services
initiate order and efficiency in these areas: filing, desk top
management, recycling, information management, storage, time
management, work-flow process. Please call for a complimentary brochure.

AUSTIN, JAFRA
Cubbyholes Unlimited
41 Sutter Street, Suite 1702
San Francisco, CA 94104-4903
800-476-8085 Pager 415-560-5578

•   Small spaces and big messes are my specialty. I listen closely and help you create a system, true to who you are, that keeps you organized and uses what's already at hand so that it works for you. Free intro/follow-up consultations. Recession rates. 35 years experience. Satisfaction guaranteed.

AUSTIN, PAMELA SMALL
Organization By Design
575 West College Avenue, Suite 101-A
Santa Rosa, CA 95401
707-544-6340 FAX 707-576-8190

• +   I specialize in the process of organization. My business is to help your business run more efficiently with simple yet effective systems. I help to "re-engineer" new infrastructure which supports your company's growth. The customized systems are easy-to-use, allow rapid access of information and provide continuity throughout an organization.

BARRERA, SUE
Office-Right
1819 Virginia Street
Berkeley, CA 94703
510-843-5918 FAX 510-843-5950

•   "A place for everything and everything in its place" applies to any environment--file cabinet, desk, office, storage unit. I help clients eliminate the overwhelmed feeling that dis-organization causes, provide home/business office organizing, orchestrate relocations and create self-maintaining systems tailored to the needs of small businesses, self-employed professionals and individuals.

BASKAY, TUDI
Time To Organize
P. O. Box 1623
Alameda, CA 94501
510-521-2453

•   Time, space and paper management for businesses, professionals and homes. Consultation and hands-on. Focused on small businesses, home offices and the creative and service sectors. Solid experience working with the chronically disorganized ("Packrats"). Active member NAPO National Study Group on Chronic Disorganization.

BECHEN, KATHRYN R.
Organized With Ease
7629 Pasadena Avenue
Omaha, NE 68124
402-391-8951 FAX 402-391-0483

•   Combining practical, proven organizing and time management techniques and concepts with firm guidance, discipline, humor and empathy, Organized With Ease enables businesses and employees to "get and stay organized," increasing productivity and gaining better control over work, time and space. The firm organizes desks, paper, people, projects, filing systems and space.

BIDERMAN, ANN F.
Ann F. Biderman
P. O. Box 31568
San Francisco, CA 94131
415-661-5168

• +   Bookkeeping, organizing and consulting for small businesses and individuals. Creating and maintaining systems on MacIntosh and manually. Setting up and maintaining filing and record keeping systems.

BLACK, NANCY
Organization Plus
14 Palmer Road
Beverly, MA 01915-2710
508-922-6136 FAX 508-927-1267

+   Nancy Black specializes in business consulting and
works with individuals and businesses on goal setting, time
management and clutter control. Organization Plus is a personalized service. Unlike group seminars, you meet one-on-one
with professional organizer Nancy Black to assess, solve and
follow-through with your individual needs.

BLAIR, BETH
Organizing Specialists
3848 Duncan Place
Palo Alto, CA 94306
415-424-8643 FAX 415-424-8643

• +   Professional organizing services for your office, home
and home-based business, including paper and time management, space planning and custom filing systems. Beth Blair, Professional Organizer, will help you determine goals and priorities
for your organizing projects, then help you bring peace, calm
and a feeling of control back to your life!

BOYDSTON, DIANA
Transitions, Ltd.
P. O. Box 11156
Santa Rosa, CA 95406
707-528-6905

Implement accounting software, write procedures.
Design efficient records management systems and procedures.
Reorganize existing accounting and records management systems. Educate employers on proper procedures. Hire and train
staff in order to maximize efficiency while minimizing cost.

BRIGHT, SANDY
Bright Ideas
807 Magellan Lane
Foster City, CA 94404
415-572-0662

Sandy operates on a whole-life approach to organization and time management. She likes to look at the way people live their lives and tailor her advice for their specific needs. She'll do everything from arranging your life to planning a party to setting up files to putting your kitchen together.

CANTU, SYLVIA
Office Services for Professionals
3145 Geary, #426
San Francisco, CA 94118
415-386-8613 FAX 415-386-5205

• I love disorganization! I can't wait to roll up my sleeves and start reorganizing. My passion for organizing can help you put your business or home in order. Drawing on 12 years' experience at a Fortune 500 company, my specialty is streamlining or setting up office procedures. And yes, I do files!

CARTER, ANNABELLE B.
Professional Organizer
2029 - 9th Avenue
Oakland, CA 94606
510-645-1868 FAX 510-645-1868

Reliable, dependable and very detailed professional organizer to support individual and small businesses: setup, design, train and maintain computer systems (accounting and financial packages, spreadsheets, databases, word processors, graphics); organize and maintain papers, records, files and information; prepare income tax returns; manage cash and finances.

CARVALHO, PRISCILLA
Symmetry & Order
P. O. Box 933
El Granada, CA 94018
415-726-1933

•	Clear the clutter and clear your mind. My simple but ingenious systems will change the way you handle your time, space and paper--bringing lasting organizational solutions to your home and business life. Symmetry & Order can open the doors to greater creativity and productivity. Call today.

CAYLOR, PAIGE H.
Alternative Business Solutions
435 Petaluma Avenue, Suite 120
Sebastapol, CA 95472
707-829-3633	FAX 707-829-2938

•	Paige assists clients in all facets of office organization-- from office systems to time management. She specializes in setting up manual and computerized accounting and book- keeping systems. Her objective is to keep things simple so that transitions can be made as effortlessly as possible.

CHASINOV, ARNOLD
Organizational & Time Management Consultant
2142 - 40th Avenue
San Francisco, CA 94116
415-664-1396

•	I coach individuals to deal effectively and efficiently with information, tasks and decisions. This results in increased self-esteem and productivity and saving time, energy & money. I teach clients organization and time management skills: setting goals, planning, prioritizing, scheduling, categorizing and systematizing. Together, we create functional systems, work- spaces and living spaces.

CLARK, LUPE
Apropos
P. O. Box 2022
Danville, CA 94526
510-736-1701

Apropos specializes in "time-saving services." For example: errands, shopping, packing, unpacking, home interior organizing, etc. Whether you're relocating or just too busy to get personal things done, we can help. From the smallest errand to turn key moves, we provide consultation, leg work, recommendations and follow through.

CORONA-SUTTON, BARBARA
The Clutter Cutter
819 West Roseburg Avenue, #168
Modesto, CA 95350
209-578-0787 FAX 209-572-0502

The Clutter Cutter offers non-judgmental hands-on organizing for home and office environments. Services are tailored to accommodate the personal goals and work habits of individuals or the unique requirements of a business. All services are provided with confidentiality and integrity. A Pre-Service Consultation is required.

COVINGTON, GAYLE
Vision Marketing Services
415 East Broad Street, Suite 107
Columbus, OH 43215
614-221-5220 FAX 614-461-7987

With a motto of "Simply Organized," the business offers consulting services as well as in-house and independent training seminars and workshops--all with the aim of creating more efficient and streamlined work environments.

CRAIG, JOAN
TimeValue Organizing Services
P. O. Box 930
Concord, CA 94522-0930
510-676-0506

• I guide and support people in making choices that lead to a feeling of control over their lives and their belongings. To do this I help them implement methods and systems of organizing that they can continue on their own. My approach is non-judgmental and light-hearted.

DATA SOFT CORPORATION (Associate Member)
Samuel Hahn
2880 Zanker Road
San Jose, CA 95134
408-434-0779 FAX 408-434-0915

DataSoft develops affordable PC software that assists individuals to manage their paperwork effectively online, without the paper. Our application can be your electronic file cabinet, when used in conjunction with a document scanner.

DeBENNEDETTI, MSW, GERALDINE
Ecoculture Associates
916 Kana Place
Honolulu, HI 96816
808-734-1159 FAX 808-924-1414

Residential organizing: How to run the house when you're not there; lists for disasters, travel, inventories; how to live in a two-story house; how not to clean too often. Identification of Packrat Behavior and therapy for chronic disorganization. Help with partialization, reinforcement. Corporation Mom.

DeFOUR, CAROL
Before DeFour and After
P. O. Box 3868
Pago Pago, American Samoa 96799-3868
684-699-4800 FAX 684-699-4797

•   Before, DeFour & After hands-on professional organizing, personalized to suit your needs.

DERBES, ELYSE
Intellisearch
229 Chattanooga Street
San Francisco, CA 94114
415-648-8028

       Business management, bookkeeping, office organization,
consulting for special projects.

DeVIVO, JUDY
Altos Business Services
101 First Street, Suite 184
Los Altos, CA 94022
415-941-2272

•   Judy offers friendly support for your personal or
business financial records management. Call her to discuss
computerizing your information for tax purposes and peace of
mind. Use her Mac/PC or Yours. Get information about the
latest and best software. You can even mail your information to
her. Free consultation.

DREISBACK, MEREDITH
Time for You
9545 Westside Road
Healdsburg, CA 95448
707-433-2816

       Time for You offers home organization services ranging
from clutter control to paper management, establishing simple
systems within the client's daily routine to accomplish this goal.

DRING, DIANA
Natural Order
120 Redwood Avenue, #6
Corte Madera, CA 94925
415-924-9161

• +   I believe the best organization comes from within us when our priorities are clear and we honor them consistently. My commitment is to help you discover your own natural order, create simple systems that reflect your unique style, and support you with coaching to manage yourself and your resources more skillfully.

DUFFY, EMILY
Order From Chaos
1025 Carleton Street, #9
Berkeley, CA 94710
510-527-1449

Order From Chaos provides individualized service to meet your organizational needs at home or at work. Specialties include: filing systems, office and space planning and layout, special events planning and residential organizing. Earthquake safety planning is also available.

ELLIOTT, RHONDA
Organized By Design
5424-10 Sunol Blvd., #202
Pleasanton, CA 94566
510-426-9540

Offers services to help today's busy person gain more time and control over their life by: designing better places to work in, play in or just relax in; planning special events or meetings; setting up and/or maintaining financial record keeping; creating interesting photo albums. Special projects are always welcomed.

ENSIGN, PAULETTE
Organizing Solutions, Inc.
26 Winding Lane
Bedford Hills, NY 10507
914-666-6414 FAX 914-242-5201

+   Consulting to organizers and other small business owners on marketing and business development; seminars and publications.

FISHER, LAURA L.
Laura's Bookkeeping Services
1167 Junipero Avenue
Redwood City, CA 94061
415-365-1000 FAX 415-365-1900

I offer complete office organizing services from filing systems and desk space order to computerizing financial information and training staff. Each job is different and every client is individual in their specific needs. Together we establish goals and transform your office into a calm, efficient and organized environment.

FREID, MARSHA
In Harmony
15 South Green
Larkspur, CA 94939
415-924-5890

• +   My purpose is to empower you in your home or office so that you can provide a functional, nurturing and beautiful environment for yourself and others close to you. You will learn the basics of organizing and will thereafter have a structure to build on.

GADENER, MELANIE
Productivity Plus Processes
116 Morrison Canyon Road
Fremont, CA 94536
510-797-4660 FAX 510-797-5620

• A corporate coaching/consulting service that assists knowledge workers in becoming efficient, effective and productive. We help individuals and workteams in defining, increasing, then maintaining productivity...despite hidden or obvious obstacles. These obstacles could include increased workloads, ineffective delegation, undefined goals, procrastination or even piles of paper on a desk!

GRACIANY, LYNDA
3755 Hilltop Court
Soquel, CA 95073
408-462-6641

Increase your effectiveness and experience the advantages of order in your life. Wholistic workflow systems, including home management, paper management and filing systems, are dynamically and creatively tailored to your personal needs.

GRAVES, LINDA LENORE
Interior Spaces/The Healing Decorator
2786 Ohio Avenue
Redwood City, CA 94061
415-368-5532

• Space awareness as a tool to change your life and support the changes. Create positive energy and self-esteem in a person through awareness of the environment. Raise energy levels and spirit through beauty, organization, functionality and personal heritage in home/business environments. Incorporating Feng Shui. Speaking/workshops available.

GROSS-CERF, LYNN
Organization...and More!
467 Saratoga Avenue, Suite 11
San Jose, CA 95129
408-266-3339 FAX 408-266-3339

Customized organizational consulting for your business or home! Specializing in: analyzing your work flow, selecting necessary systems or controls, creating plans and procedures, developing time management strategies. By implementing these techniques you will create: more productivity, additional control, free time, less stress.

GURSE, ROBIN
931-A Liberty Street
El Cerrito, CA 94530
510-524-0508

• + Specializing in time and project management, Robin assists clients in creating a vision for their project. She then coaches her clients in the specific steps of: goal setting, support, accountability, acknowledgment and rest/play. Robin consults to businesses and individuals. She also conducts workshops and leads support groups on "overcoming procrastination."

HANSELL, RUTH
Transition Support Services
P. O. Box 786
Cotati, CA 94931
707-664-0960

My work is for people who are undergoing changes in their lives. I provide organizational systems that increase effectiveness and clear away clutter. By organizing time, space and events, transition is made more manageable and less stressful.

HEIECK, VALERIE
Organize Me, Please!
P. O. Box 620359
Woodside, CA 94062
415-854-2821 FAX 415-854-2090

I assist people in organizing their home and/or office. I also help people set personal and/or business goals and then work with them to achieve those goals!

HEMPHILL, BARBARA
Hemphill & Associates, Inc.
1464 Garner Station Blvd., #330
Raleigh, NC 27603-3634
919-834-8510 FAX 919-834-8570

+ Author of Kiplinger's <u>Taming the Paper Tiger</u>. Custom presentations, training programs, and consultation to assist individuals and organizations identify and implement systems for desktop management, paper and computer filing systems. Topics include "On a Clear Day You Can See Your Desktop!" and "Caging the Paper Tiger: Filing Systems That Work!"

HIGGINS, LAURA
Turning Point
37 Truman Drive
Novato, CA 94947
415-898-0053 FAX 415-892-0072

• Prepare for a life change! Moving? Redecorating? Overwhelmed? Banish chaos and clutter from your home. We specialize in making life transitions more enjoyable, less stressful. Experience the "treasure hunt" process of sifting through your belongings to keep and showcase your treasures, releasing the items which are no longer you.

HURLBUT, SUSAN
HTO Enterprises, Inc.
P. O. Box 1703
Clackamas, OR 97015
800-225-8755 FAX 503-653-1059

\+   Producers/distributors of audio and video "how to
organize" training products. First release: "How To Organize
Your Desk."

JOHNSON, PAT
Pat's Medical Insurance Counseling
1715 Christina Drive
Los Altos, CA   94024
415-967-0636 FAX 415-965-2440

We organize the medical insurance part of clients' lives--
by handling their claims, billing problems, letting them know
what they owe. We obtain the full benefit they are entitled to. In
addition we do policy analysis and comparison. With personal
attention we focus on continuity and quality of service.

JONES, KARLA
Get Organized
1714 Lake Street
San Mateo, CA 94403
415-573-8560

•   Reduce stress, simplify your life, get organized with Get
Organized. Hands on help to eliminate chaos in your office,
files, kitchen, closet, garage, personal papers or family records.
Working together we can de-clutter your environment and
create a plan to keep you organized. Free quarterly tips
newsletter to clients.

JOSEPH, CONSTANCE C.
Family Systems
2428 Baggett Drive
Santa Rosa, CA 95401
707-576-1353

Family Systems provides consulting and hands-on organization for all aspects of family living--from creating systems for information management (personal documents, family history, emergency information) to space management (office, kitchen, bedroom, storage, garage, your room), to everyday living management (scheduling appointments and task assignments, earthquake readiness, address books).

KAISER, MELANIE
Systems in Order S.I.O.
P. O. Box 3133
Rohnert Park, CA 94927
707-578-1459

Inter-office organization--includes: file system setups and records management; time management counseling; inter-office relating skills pertaining to productivity and rate of turnover; cash flow management/budgets for personal or home use; bookkeeping; and office supply service.

KAMPE, CAROL
Business Arts Associates
2404 California Street, #35
San Francisco, CA 94115
415-922-0207

• I help businesses and individuals out of the clutter trap by creating systems to control paper, space and time more effectively.

KANE, EA, CAROLE
Organizational Consultant
6200 Irma Avenue
El Cerrito, CA 94530
510-234-7075 FAX 510-234-8656

• + Dedicated to increasing your peace of mind, leisure time and wealth! Helping people to set goals and create action plans. Providing time and project management, paperflow systems and spacial organization for businesses and homes. Setting up and maintaining accounting systems and preparing current and prior years tax returns.

KAYE, BEV
Resources Unlimited
2905 Carolina Avenue
Redwood City, CA 94061
415-366-1869

I am committed to keeping your "free" time free. I will do anything you don't have time to do, don't like to do or can't do because of a physical limitation or time limitation. I will do one-time projects or on-going projects.

KLEINBERG, VERONICA
Clutterbusters Organizing Services
780 Elizabeth Street
San Francisco, CA 94114
415-282-4412

• I offer organizing services for individuals and businesses which include setting up and maintaining easy access filing systems, recordkeeping, space planning and personal support. For people with too much to do and too little time to do it, I can manage your clutter and help reduce the feeling of being overwhelmed by paper.

KNEUBUHL, ALLISON
TimeLines
P. O. Box 82
Moraga, CA 94556
510-376-1720

TimeLines is designed to help you with your busy life through personalized consultation. By applying principles of time and organizational management to your everyday activities, I can increase your productivity and save you money while giving you the gift of extra time to do the things that are important to you.

KRAUSS, DENISE
System Development
771 Olive Court
San Bruno, CA 94066
415-588-2027

System Development specializes in small and home-based business office systems and procedures. A complete paper and workflow structure is put in place to give the business a foundation from which to work. System Development is also strong in clutter control, event planning and general residential organization. Maintenance contracts available.

KRISTENSEN, SHARON
Organization Plus ®
801 Cotton Street
Menlo Park, CA 94025
415-328-7475

• +   Organization Plus offers Organizing Services and Personal Effectiveness Coaching focusing on the organization process; organizing fundamentals; achieving goals; management of desk, paper, projects, space and time; workplace productivity and effectiveness. Provides on-site consulting, coaching, hands-on services and workshops for business and home.

LANE, CELESTE
A Matter of Organization
433 Town Center, #661
Corte Madera, CA 94925
415-257-8291

•   A Matter of Organization specializes in organizing law offices. After a consultation to determine an attorney's individual style and goals, the office is analyzed. Systems such as collections, conflict checks, filing and closed file retrieval are restructured as needed. Administrative duties are streamlined, allowing more time to practice law.

LANGAN, ELLEN
Langan & Associates
P. O. Box 19504
Seattle, WA 98119
206-284-1482

+   A company dedicated to helping individuals and businesses get organized and stay organized. We provide business and home consulting, in-house seminars and speakers. Products include problem definition, needs assessment, systems design and implementation, spatial design, clutter control, time and paper management and creative and practical solutions.

LARSEN, KAREN
Organizing Unlimited
900 North Rancho Road
El Sobrante, CA 94803
510-222-3434 FAX 510-222-5045

•   In offices I organize filing systems, records, archives, space, storage, supplies, systems, procedures and inventories. In homes I organize paperwork, filing systems, children's rooms, closets and garages. Direct benefits are: create time, increase productivity, gain space, smooth work flow, reduce stress, save money and create a harmonious environment to live/work in.

LARSEN, LEE VICTORIA
Time, Paper & Cash Management Services
P. O. Box 983
Mill Valley, CA 94942
415-381-3284 FAX 415-332-5969

• + First, we write goals and second, we prioritize them. Then, collaboratively, we design the method for managing the highest priority goals/projects. In all cases, this includes listing items-to-do then integrating these realistically into clients' calendars. For time, paper and/or cash management support, systems are tailored to suit each client.

LAYER, CHRISTINE R.
Chaos Control
13902 Fiji Way, Suite 218
Marina del Rey, CA 90292
310-822-8805

• Provide home and office organizing services with an emphasis on paper management, filing systems setup and clutter control. Create functional financial and recordkeeping systems. Extensive experience in tax preparation and with health, auto and life insurance claims. Organizational skills training available. Specialize in the Entertainment Industry. Dependability and confidentiality guaranteed.

LEINOW, D. TERUMI O.
Terumi & Associates
P. O. Box 154
Woodacre, CA 94973
415-488-4580 FAX 415-488-4886

I am a Creative Organizer who brings sanity and sanctity into the work place! Together we will transform your office into a sacred "temple" by designing effective office systems/procedures and by creating an inspiring workspace.

LESOWITZ, MIKKI
Divine Order
8944 Dicks Street
West Hollywood, CA 90069
310-271-5957 FAX 310-271-5957

Divine Order provides professional organizing services primarily to a residential and small business clientele. The company's scope of services is vast and varied and includes space, time and paper management.

LETH, LEE R.
The Knowledge Organizer
17735 Elm Avenue
Morgan Hill, CA 95037-2901
408-778-5875 CompuServe: 73233,2534

Your most valuable belonging is Time! I have PC computer tools to help you save time. From orientation seminars through brainstorming workshops, I will help you clarify your problems and needs, and then implement solutions for converting your raw business information into relevant, timely knowledge.

LEVENSON, EDIE
Asset Trackers
P. O. Box 3077
Culver City, CA 90230
310-202-0293 FAX 310-202-0294

+ Computer consulting and training. Complete small business set-up and training on your Mac or PC. Computer records management service, including business and personal finances, client lists, address books, home inventories, collectibles, bibliographies, etc. Formatted for your personal organizer, 3-ring binder, rolodex or permanently bound. Mail-order services available.

LILLIAN VERNON CATALOG (Associate Member)
Lillian Vernon Corporation
Virginia Beach, VA 23479
800-285-5555 FAX 804-430-1010

• +   Lillian Vernon catalogs have hundreds of products to help you get and stay organized. Discounts are available on large quantities--over 24 pieces of an item. Catalogs are free of charge upon request.

LIPTON, LINDA J.
Linda J. Lipton, Marketing and Graphics
24 Corrillo Drive
San Rafael, CA 94903
415-479-9349 FAX 415-507-0555

•   Marketing and Graphic Design services--specializing in product development, packaging, catalog and manual organization and design, newsletter design and production. Manufacturer of the Komfort Grip ® and Big Gripper™, foam rubber grips for tools.

LIVELY, JENNIFER
Professional Organizer
1882 35th Avenue
San Francisco, CA 94122
415-566-9733

I am committed to assisting clients in having more control over their time, reducing their stress and increasing their productivity. My services include organizing the home and home office by providing anti-clutter systems, filing systems, paper and records management and bookkeeping systems.

LONTZ, DAVID
The Organization Man
P. O. Box 530
Novato, CA 94948
415-898-2713

I help people become organized so they have more efficient use of time, space and resources. By being able to locate what they already have, they can reduce frustration and redundancy, eliminate clutter and ultimately reduce the environmental impact of each family's life.

LOX, HESTER
Painless Paperwork Productions
1085 South Van Ness, #104
San Francisco , CA 94110
415-282-8650

•   Singles ads, alumnae newsletters, your June '90 phone bill, garden supply catalogs, your mother's will and a great line from Seinfeld all in a heap on the closet floor or, worse, the kitchen table? Dig out, make a real place for everything, create sanity and have peace in your home.

LUTHER, JOHANNA
Family Packers
6116 Merced Avenue, #165
Oakland, CA 94611
510-893-6896

•   Johanna Luther and Janna C. Luther, a mother/daughter team, are partners in Family Packers. They provide expert packing services for people who are moving home or office. They also provide unpacking services, remove and recycle all packing debris, leaving everything neat, orderly and in its proper place.

MacKENZIE, SUSAN H.
Project Management Services
15 Acorn Way
Kentfield, CA 94904
415-461-5379

Specializes in projects which involve the organization of ideas, information and resources. Particular areas of focus include meeting planning and facilitation, the planning and execution of special events and writing and editing of reports, newsletters, etc.

MADVIG, KEVEN
Simply Organized
P. O. Box 5031
Larkspur, CA 94977-5031
415-461-1300

• Simply Organized provides organizing services for households, home offices and small businesses, emphasizing clutter control, paper handling, storage planning (closets, kitchens, garages) and time management.

MAGORIAN, KAREN
Tahoe Organizing and Financial Services
P. O. Box 7191
Incline Village, NV 89452
702-831-6259 FAX 702-831-7760

• + I help people to organize their businesses and their homes. With twenty years of accounting experience and extensive PC computer experience, my emphasis is on design and maintenance of accounting, filing and paperflow systems; office organization; business management; space utilization; inventories; relocation assistance and computer consulting.

MARRS, DEBRA
PathShapers
127 Imperio Avenue
Fremont, CA 94539
510-770-0641

Specializing in time management and organization for business. Personal coaching and workshops in goal setting, time management, overcoming procrastination and life balance. A messy desk, an overbooked calendar or a bad case of procrastination? We will show you how to gain 1-2 extra hours productive time per day, handle paperwork efficiently and work in a clutter-free office.

MARTIN, LESLIE K.
7740 Squirehill Court
Cupertino, CA 95014
408-446-3254 E-Mail:lmartin@aol.com

• Need a story told? Leslie K. Martin helps businesses answer such questions as: What are we trying to say and how should we say it? Her corporate communications include employee manuals, internal communiqués, product, people and business profiles and press releases. What's your story?

MARTIN, PATRICIA
Master Plan
2600 Union Street, Suite 204
San Francisco, CA 94123
415-749-0399

MATHIS, ELLEN P.
Organizing Services
63 St. Joseph Avenue
Long Beach, CA 90803-3158
310-433-6509

Organizing Services specializes in working with individuals to help them get organized so that they manage their work space, not allowing it to manage them.

McARTHUR, SUSAN
McArthur Office Management Services
P. O. Box 2425
Mill Valley, CA 94942
415-388-4950

McArthur Office Management Services provides creative organizational solutions to the small business owner. Services include office management on an as-needed basis (weekly, bi-weekly); file management; tracking client expenses; bill paying; managing bank accounts; computer training and computer purchasing advice.

MERRIMAN, M.Ed., ELIZABETH
Methods by Merriman
40 Greenwood Bay Drive
Tiburon, CA 94920
415-383-3318

Coaching to provide focus, direction and support as you move beyond obstacles to experiencing success. Clients achieve greater balance that brings accomplishment and a sense of well-being. Services include: organization of your workspace and paper flow, personally designed planning notebooks and systems and Organization, Time Management and Motivational Seminars.

METZ, KATHERINE
The Art of Placement
43 Grand Boulevard
San Mateo, CA 94401
415-348-7822 FAX 415-348-7822

• + Feng Shui, practiced with an eye for beauty, a spirit for healing and a bit of uncommon sense. Combining the art of Feng Shui and the science of Bau-biologie to create healthy homes and workplaces.

MILLER, KERRY
Everything in its Place
600 34th Avenue, Apt. 2
San Francisco, CA 94121
415-751-6619

At Everything in its Place we believe everything has its place--including your individual needs. We creatively solve your problems by listening to your frustrations and customizing a system for you. We save you time and money because being organized increases productivity. Let Everything in its Place create a unique system for unique you.

MYRRHA, ANACARIA
Simple Systems
32 Narragansett Cove
San Rafael, CA 94901-4476
415-454-9343

• +   Anacaria Myrrha offers non-judgmental support to help people become self-sufficient, productive and satisfied. She specializes in Information, Paper and Energy Management Systems—filing, paper and workflow, and planning notebooks—with attention to personal priorities, patterns and styles. Considerate, thoughtful service since 1977, confidentiality guaranteed, excellent references. Free telephone consultation.

NEWSOM, OLINDA G.

Design by Olinda	**Design by Olinda**
1001 Olive Street	1705 Gum Street
Menlo Park, CA 94025	San Mateo, CA 94402
415-321-7525	415-570-7958

By reorganizing and rearranging your existing furnishings and keepsakes, I can creatively transform and create a desirable fresh new look!

O'CONNOR, CANDICE
Candice O'Connor Professional Organizing
P. O. Box 813
Aptos, CA 95001
408-477-9027

"Everything has a home and every home has a thing." Once this concept is understood, a stress-free environment is yours. Together, we will create systems that work for you. You will learn how to successfully manage your environment so peace, harmony and organization will reign--not clutter and chaos.

PAUKER, GLORIA
ClutterBuddies
20929-47 Ventura Blvd., Suite 448
Woodland Hills, CA 91364
818-886-6830

I am a special education teacher who organizes children with learning disabilities. I help them organize their time and schoolwork. I work with them on special projects. I also work with adults who are chronically disorganized (ADD residual).

PLAKUN, SCOTT
Productive Strategies
44 Montgomery Street, Suite 500
San Francisco, CA 94104
415-955-0506

• Productive Strategies is the local representative of the Self-Management System, which combines proven training with an advanced notebook organizer to guarantee a 20% to 40% increase in productivity.

POER, KATHLEEN
Spacial Design
21 Pamaron Way, Suite A
Novato, CA 94949
415-382-1218   FAX 415-382-1233

• +   Spacial Design provides consultation, design, working
drawings, cabinetry and equipment and installation of systems
and centers for the kitchen, office, garage and closets. Their
work has received national acclaim. Kathleen Poer, designer,
trainer and organizational specialist, has been sharing her
expertise with others for more than 12 years.

POLLAR, ODETTE
Time Management Systems
1441 Franklin Street, Suite 310
Oakland, CA 94612
510-763-8482 FAX 510-835-8531

• +   Odette Pollar directs the training firm Time Management Systems, offering seminars, consulting and writing on
organization, time management and planning. She is the author
of the book *Organizing Your Work Space: A Guide to Personal
Productivity*.

PRINCE, TERRY
Organized & Loving It, Associates
6409 Fuego Way
Elk Grove, CA 95758
916-684-1401

• +   Paper management specialist for office and home. Seminars on organizational topics. Writer.

RALEIGH, BARBARA
Clutter ..... Be Gone
10301 Alpine Drive, Suite 1
Cupertino, CA 95014
408-732-0740

•   Barbara is a teacher, coach and motivator who assists her
clients in achieving their organizing goals and develops a personal organizing system for each client. She organizes homes,
desks/work spaces, paperwork and projects, assists in the
settling of estates, writes procedure and personnel manuals and
conducts seminars.

READ, CLAUDIA
Getting Organized
2059 South Macon Way
Aurora, CO 80014
303-755-7867

+   Getting Organized is a solution to the problems which
seem to steal your time, drain your energy and overwhelm your
lifestyle. Adapting to each unique individual, we provide
hands-on service which categorizes, prioritizes and systematizes
your personal and professional life in order to establish and
maintain an efficient system for maximum productivity.

REIS, KAREN
Creative Memories
662 Princeton Drive
Sunnyvale, CA 94087
408-720-1069

Teach classes and hold workshops on how to preserve
photographs and memorabilia. How to get started now, organizing and album page ideas. Also supply archival materials to
create wonderful albums for enjoyment now and in the future.

RICKS, ALLISON
Ascending Order
P. O. Box 577
San Leandro, CA 94577
510-614-0770

• Ascending Order offers organizing assistance to individuals and small businesses. Services, tailored to meet the client's needs, include residential, office, special project and personal organizing. Special attention is given to the optimal combination of the functional and the aesthetically pleasing.

ROETHE, T. J.
Organization...Designed for You
P. O. Box 3164
Walnut Creek, CA 94598
510-937-0396

• Time management and organization seminars/workshops/training. Keynote speaker helps you put more time and fun in your life. Hands-on organization of offices, homes and individuals. Beautifies and simplifies homes using existing furnishings. Records audio and video oral family histories.

ROHRBACH, ANNIE
Professional Organizer
45 Corte de Sabla
Greenbrae, CA 94904-1309
415-461-3537 FAX 415-461-3713

• + Feel better organized in your home, small business, when you are moving and/or planning special events. Receive gentle guidance and support to create surroundings that are more comfortable and orderly, so you feel more relaxed and can live your life more fully. Specialties include space planning and de-cluttering. Since 1987.

ROSSOW, MARY E.
Rossow Resources
334 State Street, Suite 307
Los Altos, CA 94022
415-969-4939

Rossow Resources
2715 Sherman Street, Suite 3
Eau Claire, WI 54701
715-831-1733

• +   Purveyors of organizational consulting...business and home management services. Client advocate, coaching and life planning, resource specialist and expediter, workshops, seminars and keynote speeches, "funnrai$er" extraordinaire. Side dish of non-judgmental, empathetic support included at no extra charge.

ROSSUM, KAREN M.
Personal Organization Consultant
102 Los Lomas Drive
Aptos, CA 95003-3221
408-688-2550 FAX 408-688-5180

• +   Hands-on reorganization of office environments. Individualized coaching in the use of organization tools and techniques that focus on integrity of organization--developing the habits and routines that keep organization in place.

SACKS, MBA, S. LYNN MORTIMER
Clutter Clinic
351 N. Newport Blvd., Suite 357
Newport Beach, CA 92663
714-722-1225 FAX 714-650-9210

Dear Clutter Clinic:
Clyde and I used to climb over clutter without a clue for clearing it out. It was closing in, and we were close to clobbering each other. You reclaimed clearings by clarifying, clustering and classifying and we clap to your cleverness, class and clemency!!
--Clara Client

SAGAL, JAN
The Paper Wizard
P. O. Box 404
Auburn, CA 95604
916-885-4701 FAX 916-885-4701

•   The Paper Wizard assists individuals and organizations streamline day-to-day business operations. By assessing your needs, we'll develop practical, timesaving paperwork systems, design and implement customized filing systems and create a functional working environment through efficient space utilization.

SAUNDERS, SUZANNE O.
SOS Organizational Services
P. O. Box 1435
Mill Valley, CA   94942-1435
415-456-4-SOS

      SOS Organizational Services will do more than help you keep your head above water. Suzanne Saunders specializes in home office organization and time management and offers a broad selection of other services. She will carefully consider your needs in order to customize systems that are both pleasing and practical.

SCHECHTER, HARRIET
The Miracle Worker Organizing Service
3368 Governor Drive, Suite F-199
San Diego, CA 92122
619-581-1241 FAX 619-450-3680

+   Specializing in clutter control and curing "paperosis displacea" since 1986, The Miracle Worker helps individuals, businesses and organizations achieve control of time, space and paper by providing the following services: design and set-up of customized paper-flow and filing systems; organizational consulting and hands-on organizing; seminars, workshops and training programs.

SCHOMP, GRETCHEN
Bring to Order
87 Nelson Avenue
Mill Valley, CA 94941
415-381-0129 FAX 415-388-5850

• Bring to Order works with you to bring organization and continuity into your daily life according to your individual needs. Together we develop a plan of action and go to work! Whether it be goal and priority setting, time or paper management or workplace design, Bring to Order can help you make the idea of "getting organized" a reality!

SCHWARTZ, ZOE
EuroFiles, Division of Bindertek
2656 Bridgeway, P. O. Box 806
Sausalito, CA 94965
415-332-8688 FAX 415-332-2641

The EuroFiles system of easy-to-use, high quality ring binders and index tab dividers make paperwork quick to file and easy to find. Space-efficient shelving and rotary carousels save up to 70% of valuable floor space. Ideal for project files, departmental or central files and company manuals. Call for our catalog.

SCORDINO, JoANN
Organize for Action
1935 Franklin St., #502
San Francisco, CA 94109
415-474-9140

• + Provide business and personal organizational services along with special events/projects. We organize anything from a child's room to a corporate department filing system to large fundraising events.

SHANKLE, SUSAN
Professional Organizer
3182 Campus Drive, #364
San Mateo, CA 94403
415-574-2301 FAX 415-574-3750

Home office set-up, reorganize storage and work spaces, photographic inventories and transform saved stuff into useful tools and information. Authored "The Joy of Carpooling," a how-to booklet for getting started with ridesharing to save time, money and stress.

SKIBITZKE, JUDY
JS Associates
809 B Cuesta Drive, Suite 192
Mountain View , CA 94040
415-694-7979 FAX 415-960-6860

JS Associates is committed to planning and designing environments which support individuals and organizations to get their jobs done. Services include space planning, interior design, computer aided design (CAD) services, project management and relocation management.

SMITH, JEANNE K.
Exit, Stage Right
P. O. Box 60794
Palo Alto, CA 94306
415-493-3948

Estate organization = Exit, this Stage the Right way. Using original materials, Jeanne creates a strategic game plan to enable her clients to handle the practical, administrative issues of death. Although pre-need planning is emphasized, Jeanne is there to walk you and your family through this crisis. She also gives presentations to groups interested in this gift of love.

STANFORD, ALICE
Design Focus
918 Bel Marin Keys Blvd.
Novato, CA 94949
415-883-1104

• +   Design Focus, functional and distinctive interiors. Staging: Getting ready to sell your home? Design: Redecorating? Planning to move? Organizing: Eliminate chaos, clutter and guilt.

STELTER, SANDY
1314 Pintail Drive
Suisun, CA 94585
707-426-3729

STEPHENS, PATRICK
When In Doubt, Get Organized!
1330 Old West Drive
Sacramento, CA 95834-1411
916-927-4869

I specialize in personal and business record keeping systems, with an extensive background in accounting, internal auditing, budget analysis, technical writing and operations analysis. These skills are combined with a flexible, outgoing, fun-loving personality that serves as a catalyst in enabling you to get out of the "organizing doldrums."

STIVERS, JANE
Jane Stivers Organizing Services
8682 Phoenix Avenue
Fair Oaks, CA 95628
916-966-0889

Specializing in home offices.

STRASSMAN, FRANCES
More Than Order
6925 Snake Road
Oakland, CA 94611
510-287-5583

More Than Order is a service for taking charge of life through applying the deep principles and practices of organization. Freedom can be gained and anxiety levels gently lowered through de-cluttering space, time, mind and emotions. For small businesses and homes. Background: a lifetime of this work.

STRAUSS, MA, RCA, CAROLYN
Rainbow's End Design
5007 Rainbow's End
Culver City, CA 90230
310-841-2330 FAX 818-360-6753

I analyze the working environment for individuals and small companies and design systems that make the most efficient use of space, with or without the implementation of high technology. My designs take serious consideration towards esthetics and, with over 15 years experience in the Fine Arts, I happily recommend artwork as well as color specifications, to create optimal conditions towards comfort and productivity.

STREICH, DOROTHY I.
Organizational Consultant
3582 Jomar Drive
Napa, CA 94558
707-255-9509

Create/develop/organize file systems: eliminate clutter, provide effective and orderly storage and retrieval methods for your important documents. Manage special projects/events; plan, coordinate, facilitate project elements. Coach time management techniques: identify/maintain your priorities, gain a sense of control and reduce stress. Over 25 years of experience.

SUTHERLAND, GEORGIA L.
Family Treasures
10184 Potters Hatch
Cupertino, CA 95014
408-446-1612 FAX 415-694-3218

• "Find chaos and organize it!" has been my motto for many years. I provide writing and organizing services for personal and family memoirs, histories, photographs, genealogical information, collections, closets, junk rooms and garages. Skills and experience also include project management, desktop publishing, creating directories of organizations and planning and conducting meetings and events.

THOMSON, JUDY
Let's Get Organized
P. O. Box 7778
Fremont, CA 94537
510-793-6828

• + For those who would like to organize their office or a project within the office, we assist in setting goals, providing the impetus to get started, the continuity to complete the work and guidelines for maintenance. The methods used are unique to each client's particular needs.

TOM, JANET
Office to Order
3668 - 18th Street
San Francisco, CA 94110
415-864-5487

• + I specialize in working with filmmakers, writers, artists and other freelancers inundated by paper. By organizing their files and paper based on how they think, my clients can handle mail, manage information and find what they need quickly and easily. I also organize the work space to be efficient.

TURITTO, KATHLEEN
Office Systems Organization
P. O. Box 7762
Stockton, CA 95267-0762
209-474-2186

I reorganize office systems for established businesses. I show new entrepreneurs how to set up information storage and retrieval systems. Writing office procedure manuals, customizing forms, my specialties.

VANDER LANS, NANCY
Nancy Vander Lans
25 Willow Road, #51
Menlo Park, CA 94025
415-324-2031

I specialize in creating systems based on the individual needs and priorities of people and organizations resulting in less stress and more time and space.

VELASQUEZ, SHERRI C.
The Organization Answer
53 Larkspur Street
American Canyon, CA 94589
707-552-0760

Professional organizing services designed to provide clients with effective answers to their personal and work needs. Specializing in residential and office organizing, as well as effective methods to organize your job search. In addition, professional seminars and/or training provided to groups upon request.

VOORSANGER, JUNE
In-Line Systems
3145 Octavia Street, #14
San Francisco, CA 94123
415-922-8296

• I create filing systems to work with an individual's personal life style or an organization's functional style which allows them to flow in more harmonious rhythm and/or to accomplish specific goals.

WALLACE, ANGELA F.
Wallace Associates
20 Sunnyside Avenue A132
Mill Valley, CA 94941
415-383-8387

• Wallace Associates offers individuals and businesses personal attention, clear-sighted analyses, innovative solutions and hands-on management. Services include strategic planning; organization of business/office systems; procedures analysis and development; project development and management; and small group facilitation. Angela Wallace has over 20 years experience in small business development and management.

WATKINS, SHARRON
Organization Plus
P. O. Box 1201
Chester, CA 96020
916-259-3310

I enjoy sharing my knowledge of organizing time, information and space. I can show you how to effectively accomplish more in 24 hours, reach your goals, gain more space and store less stuff. And as a Professional Bookkeeper, I provide complete financial services.

WEGENAST, CAROL
ASAP Enterprises
P. O. Box 3076
Redwood City, CA 94064
415-365-8804 FAX 415-365-8804

I was born organized. Let me help you with: meeting and event planning--office and home (including small business exposure, seminars, theme parties and garage/estate sales). I can do research, advertising, promotion, public relations and time management to make you a great success! Call me today; I could organize a tornado!

WESTCOTT, ARLEEN
Full Agenda
616 Ninth Avenue
San Francisco, CA 94118
415-751-2166

• +   Full Agenda provides office and residential organizing services to individuals who want simplicity, efficiency and control of their paper, time and space. Working one-on-one to understand your goals, priorities and style, Arleen develops a system to effectively manage incoming information; daily, monthly and long-range planning; filing and storage systems; and space utilization.

For updated Directory information and additions, contact:

NAPO-SFBA Chapter Business Office
1592 Union Street, Suite 721
San Francisco, CA 94123
415-281-5681

MEMBERSHIP
SUMMARY
CHART

Services Provided
and
Areas Served

SFBA CHAPTER NATIONAL ASSOCIATION OF PROFESSIONAL ORGANIZERS DIRECTORY OF MEMBERS	Accounting/Bookkeeping/Financial	Health Insurance Claims	Computer Consulting/Training	Office Organizing	Residential Organizing	Paperflow/Workflow Systems	Filing Systems	Procedures Manuals	Records Management	Calendars/Planning Notebooks	Time Management/Goal Setting	Project Management	Event/Meeting Planning	Space Planning	Recycling Systems	Kitchen Design/Organizing	Closet Design/Organizing	Garage Design/Organizing
Abbott, Eve 510-528-4950	•	•		•	•	•	•		•		•		•	•				•
Albrecht, Nancy 510-773-4640				•	•	•	•		•		•	•						
Albrecht, Susie 415-775-6659				•	•													
Allen, Rick 203-775-6565			•	•		•	•			•	•							
Anderson, Mary G 415-960-3772				•	•	•	•	•		•	•	•					•	•
Aurich, Alan 415-661-3405				•	•	•	•	•		•	•	•	•	•	•		•	
Austin, Jafra 800-476-8085				•	•	•	•	•						•		•	•	•
Austin, Pamela Small 707-544-6340				•		•	•		•	•	•							
Barrera, Sue 510-843-5918	•	•		•	•		•	•	•	•		•		•		•	•	
Baskay, Tudi 510-521-2453				•	•	•	•				•			•				
Bechen, Kathryn R. 402-391-8951				•		•	•	•		•	•	•						
Biderman, Ann F. 415-661-5168	•		•	•	•		•		•					•		•		
Black, Nancy 508-922-6136		•		•	•	•	•		•	•	•	•		•		•		

Provided										Counties or Areas Served												Other
Garage/Estate Sales	Pack/Move/Relocate	Books/Libraries	Memorabilia/Photographs	Packrats/Chronic Disorganization	Errands/Personal Shopping	Seminars/Training	Speaking	Writing/Publishing	Manufacturer/Supplier	Alameda	Contra Costa	Marin	Mendocino	Napa	Sacramento	San Francisco	San Mateo	Santa Clara	Santa Cruz	Solano	Sonoma	
•	•			•	•	•	•	•		•	•	•			•		•					
					•					•	•					•						
					•					•	•	•				•	•					
						•	•															Metro N.Y. & New England
		•		•		•	•	•								•	•	•				
		•			•	•	•	•				•		•		•	•					Relocation destinations
	•	•	•			•	•	•								•	•					
			•			•	•			•	•	•	•	•	•	•				•	•	
	•	•	•	•	•					•	•	•				•						
		•	•	•		•	•	•		•	•	•				•	•	•				Los Angeles
		•	•			•	•	•														Omaha area, Nationally
					•					•	•	•				•	•					Will travel
		•	•	•																		MA: Essex, Middlesex & Suffolk Co.

SFBA CHAPTER / NATIONAL ASSOCIATION OF PROFESSIONAL ORGANIZERS DIRECTORY OF MEMBERS	Accounting/Bookkeeping/Financial	Health Insurance Claims	Computer Consulting/Training	Office Organizing	Residential Organizing	Paperflow/Workflow Systems	Filing Systems	Procedures Manuals	Records Management	Calendars/Planning Notebooks	Time Management/Goal Setting	Project Management	Event/Meeting Planning	Space Planning	Recycling Systems	Kitchen Design/Organizing	Closet Design/Organizing	Garage Design/Organizing
Blair, Beth 415-424-8643				•	•	•	•	•	•	•	•	•		•	•	•	•	•
Boydston, Diana 707-528-6905	•		•		•	•	•	•	•	•	•							
Bright, Sandy 415-572-0662		•		•	•	•	•	•		•	•		•			•	•	•
Cantu, Sylvia 415-386-8613				•	•	•	•	•	•	•	•	•						
Carter, Annabelle B. 510-645-1868	•		•	•		•	•		•			•	•					
Carvalho, Priscilla 415-726-1933				•	•	•	•	•	•		•	•				•	•	•
Caylor, Paige H. 707-829-3633	•		•	•		•					•							
Chasinov, Arnold 415-664-1396				•	•	•	•	•	•	•	•	•		•	•	•	•	•
Clark, Lupe 510-736-1701				•												•	•	•
Corona-Sutton, Barbara 209-578-0787				•	•	•	•		•					•		•	•	•
Covington, Gayle 614-221-5220				•		•	•	•				•						
Craig, Joan 510-676-0506				•	•	•	•					•	•	•		•	•	•
DataSoft Corporation 408-434-0779				•	•	•	•		•									

Provided										Counties or Areas Served												Other
Garage/Estate Sales	Pack/Move/Relocate	Books/Libraries	Memorabilia/Photographs	Packrats/Chronic Disorganization	Errands/Personal Shopping	Seminars/Training	Speaking	Writing/Publishing	Manufacturer/Supplier	Alameda	Contra Costa	Marin	Mendocino	Napa	Sacramento	San Francisco	San Mateo	Santa Clara	Santa Cruz	Solano	Sonoma	
		•	•	•		•	•		•								•	•	•			
												•	•	•						•	•	
•	•	•	•	•		•	•			•	•	•				•	•	•	•			New York City
			•							•	•	•				•	•					
			•		•					•	•	•		•		•	•	•		•	•	For special projects
	•															•						
											•			•							•	
	•	•	•	•		•	•			•	•	•				•	•					National, International
	•				•					•	•											
	•																					Stanislaus & San Joaquin Counties
						•	•															Ohio
•										•	•					•	•			•	•	
			•						•													All of USA

SFBA CHAPTER NATIONAL ASSOCIATION OF PROFESSIONAL ORGANIZERS DIRECTORY OF MEMBERS	Accounting/Bookkeeping/Financial	Health Insurance Claims	Computer Consulting/Training	Office Organizing	Residential Organizing	Paperflow/Workflow Systems	Filing Systems	Procedures Manuals	Records Management	Calendars/Planning Notebooks	Time Management/Goal Setting	Project Management	Event/Meeting Planning	Space Planning	Recycling Systems	Kitchen Design/Organizing	Closet Design/Organizing	Garage Design/Organizing
DeBenedetti, MSW, Geraldine 808-734-1159					•													•
DeFour, Carol 684-699-4800			•	•	•	•						•	•			•	•	
Derbes, Elyse 415-648-8028	•		•					•										
DeVivo, Judi 415-941-2272	•		•	•		•			•		•							
Dreisback, Meredith 707-433-2816				•	•		•		•						•	•	•	•
Dring, Diana 415-924-9161	•		•	•	•	•	•	•		•	•	•	•	•				
Duffy, Emily 510-527-1449				•	•		•	•					•	•		•	•	•
Elliott, Rhonda 510-426-9540	•		•	•	•	•	•			•	•		•	•		•	•	
Ensign, Paulette 914-666-6414																		
Fisher, Laura L. 415-365-1000	•	•	•	•			•	•		•	•	•						
Freid, Marsha 415-924-5890				•	•	•	•				•					•	•	•
Gadener, Melanie 510-797-4660				•		•	•			•	•	•	•					
Graciany, Lynda 408-462-6641				•	•	•	•		•									

Garage/Estate Sales	Pack/Move/Relocate	Books/Libraries	Memorabilia/Photographs	Packrats/Chronic Disorganization	Errands/Personal Shopping	Seminars/Training	Speaking	Writing/Publishing	Manufacturer/Supplier	Alameda	Contra Costa	Marin	Mendocino	Napa	Sacramento	San Francisco	San Mateo	Santa Clara	Santa Cruz	Solano	Sonoma	Other
		•	•																			Hawaii
	•		•	•	•																	Am. Samoa & So. Pacific
										•		•				•	•					
																		•	•			
			•		•	•															•	
				•		•	•			•	•	•		•		•				•	•	Phone coaching anywhere
	•									•		•										
			•				•			•	•							•				
						•	•	•														National, International
																•	•					
			•		•	•				•		•				•	•	•		•		
						•	•			•	•	•	•	•	•	•	•	•	•	•	•	All CA and National
																		•	•			

SFBA CHAPTER / NATIONAL ASSOCIATION OF PROFESSIONAL ORGANIZERS DIRECTORY OF MEMBERS	Accounting/Bookkeeping/Financial	Health Insurance Claims	Computer Consulting/Training	Office Organizing	Residential Organizing	Paperflow/Workflow Systems	Filing Systems	Procedures Manuals	Records Management	Calendars/Planning Notebooks	Time Management/Goal Setting	Project Management	Event/Meeting Planning	Space Planning	Recycling Systems	Kitchen Design/Organizing	Closet Design/Organizing	Garage Design/Organizing
Graves, Linda Lenore 415-368-5532			•	•										•		•	•	
Gross-Cerf, Lynn 408-266-3339				•	•	•	•	•	•	•	•							
Gurse, Robin 510-524-0508						•				•	•	•	•					
Hansell, Ruth 707-664-0960					•		•				•		•					
Heieck, Valerie 415-854-2821	•	•	•	•			•	•	•	•	•	•	•					
Hemphill, Barbara 919-834-8510				•		•	•											
Higgins, Laura 415-898-0053				•	•	•			•	•	•	•	•				•	•
Hurlbut, Susan 800-225-8755				•			•											
Johnson, Pat 415-967-0636		•																
Jones, Karla 415-573-8560				•	•	•	•		•	•	•	•		•	•	•	•	•
Joseph, Constance C. 707-576-1353	•	•	•	•	•	•	•		•	•		•	•	•	•	•	•	•
Kaiser, Melanie 707-578-1459	•			•		•	•		•	•	•							
Kampe, Carol 415-922-0207				•		•	•							•				

	Provided										Counties or Areas Served												Other
Garage/Estate Sales	Pack/Move/Relocate	Books/Libraries	Memorabilia/Photographs	Packrats/Chronic Disorganization	Errands/Personal Shopping	Seminars/Training	Speaking	Writing/Publishing	Manufacturer/Supplier	Alameda	Contra Costa	Marin	Mendocino	Napa	Sacramento	San Francisco	San Mateo	Santa Clara	Santa Cruz	Solano	Sonoma	
						●	●	●		●	●	●						●	●			National, International
																		●				
		●				●				●	●											
			●			●															●	Estate Organization
					●			●									●	●				
						●	●	●														National, International
●	●	●	●	●	●	●	●	●			●	●	●	●		●	●			●	●	Real Estate Staging
						●	●	●	●													Available Nationally
										●	●	●	●	●	●	●	●	●	●	●	●	All of USA
	●	●	●			●	●										●					
		●	●																		●	
														●							●	
						●	●	●								●						

SFBA CHAPTER / NATIONAL ASSOCIATION OF PROFESSIONAL ORGANIZERS DIRECTORY OF MEMBERS	Accounting/Bookkeeping/Financial	Health Insurance Claims	Computer Consulting/Training	Office Organizing	Residential Organizing	Paperflow/Workflow Systems	Filing Systems	Procedures Manuals	Records Management	Calendars/Planning Notebooks	Time Management/Goal Setting	Project Management	Event/Meeting Planning	Space Planning	Recycling Systems	Kitchen Design/Organizing	Closet Design/Organizing	Garage Design/Organizing
Kane, EA, Carole 510-234-7075	•		•	•	•	•	•	•	•	•	•	•	•	•	•	•	•	•
Kaye, Bev 415-366-1869		•		•	•	•	•		•	•	•	•	•	•	•	•	•	•
Kleinberg, Veronica 415-282-4412		•		•		•	•	•	•		•	•		•				
Kneubuhl, Allison 510-376-1720			•	•	•	•	•			•	•		•	•				
Krauss, Denise 415-588-2027				•	•	•	•			•			•					
Kristensen, Sharon 415-328-7475				•	•	•	•	•	•	•	•	•		•				
Lane, Celeste 415-257-8291				•		•	•	•	•	•	•			•				
Langan, Ellen 206-284-1482				•	•	•	•				•			•		•	•	•
Larsen, Karen 510-222-3434				•	•	•	•					•	•				•	•
Larsen, Lee Victoria 415-381-3284	•		•	•		•	•	•	•	•	•	•	•					
Layer, Christine R. 310-822-8805	•	•		•	•	•	•		•									
Leinow, D. Terumi O. 415-488-4580				•	•	•	•		•	•	•	•	•	•				
Lesowitz, Mikki 310-271-5957			•	•	•	•	•		•	•	•	•		•			•	•

Garage/Estate Sales	Pack/Move/Relocate	Books/Libraries	Memorabilia/Photographs	Packrats/Chronic Disorganization	Errands/Personal Shopping	Seminars/Training	Speaking	Writing/Publishing	Manufacturer/Supplier	Alameda	Contra Costa	Marin	Mendocino	Napa	Sacramento	San Francisco	San Mateo	Santa Clara	Santa Cruz	Solano	Sonoma	Other
	•		•	•		•	•			•	•	•	•	•	•	•	•	•	•	•	•	Los Angeles
•	•		•	•	•											•	•	•				
												•				•	•					
				•		•	•	•			•											
				•						•	•					•	•	•				
		•	•	•		•	•	•	•	•	•	•	•	•	•	•	•	•	•	•	•	All CA, National, International
										•	•	•				•	•				•	
				•		•	•	•														All WA, National
				•						•	•	•				•						
						•	•			•	•	•	•	•	•	•	•	•	•	•	•	Weddings; will travel
			•													•						Los Angeles County
						•	•			•		•				•					•	
	•	•	•			•	•	•								•						Los Angeles Co. & CT

SFBA CHAPTER — NATIONAL ASSOCIATION OF PROFESSIONAL ORGANIZERS — DIRECTORY OF MEMBERS	Services																	
	Accounting/Bookkeeping/Financial	Health Insurance Claims	Computer Consulting/Training	Office Organizing	Residential Organizing	Paperflow/Workflow Systems	Filing Systems	Procedures Manuals	Records Management	Calendars/Planning Notebooks	Time Management/Goal Setting	Project Management	Event/Meeting Planning	Space Planning	Recycling Systems	Kitchen Design/Organizing	Closet Design/Organizing	Garage Design/Organizing
Leth, Lee R. 408-778-5875			•	•		•		•		•	•							
Levenson, Edie 310-202-0293	•		•					•										
Lillian Vernon Catalog 800-285-5555				•	•											•	•	•
Lipton, Linda J. 415-479-9349								•				•						
Lively, Jennifer 415-566-9733	•			•	•		•		•							•	•	•
Lontz, David 415-898-2713		•		•	•	•	•	•	•	•	•	•		•		•	•	•
Lox, Hester 415-282-8650			•	•	•	•	•	•	•	•			•			•	•	•
Luther, Johanna 510-893-6896				•	•									•				
MacKenzie, Susan H. 415-461-5379				•							•	•	•	•		•	•	
Madvig, Keven 415-461-1300				•	•											•	•	•
Magorian, Karen 702-831-6259	•		•	•	•	•	•	•	•					•		•	•	
Marrs, Debra 510-770-0641				•		•				•	•							
Martin, Leslie K. 408-446-3254			•															

	Provided										Counties or Areas Served												Other
Garage/Estate Sales	Pack/Move/Relocate	Books/Libraries	Memorabilia/Photographs	Packrats/Chronic Disorganization	Errands/Personal Shopping	Seminars/Training	Speaking	Writing/Publishing	Manufacturer/Supplier	Alameda	Contra Costa	Marin	Mendocino	Napa	Sacramento	San Francisco	San Mateo	Santa Clara	Santa Cruz	Solano	Sonoma	
						•												•				
		•				•		•														Los Angeles
									•													All of USA
									•			•				•					•	
				•						•	•	•				•	•					
•	•		•	•	•							•									•	
•	•	•	•	•	•					•	•	•				•	•					
	•									•	•	•			•	•	•	•			•	Will travel
					•	•		•		•		•				•						
	•									•		•										
	•	•										•	•	•	•		•	•	•		•	Lake Tahoe & Reno
					•		•	•		•	•					•	•	•				
								•														Nationwide

SFBA CHAPTER

NATIONAL ASSOCIATION OF PROFESSIONAL ORGANIZERS

DIRECTORY OF MEMBERS

	Accounting/Bookkeeping/Financial	Health Insurance Claims	Computer Consulting/Training	Office Organizing	Residential Organizing	Paperflow/Workflow Systems	Filing Systems	Procedures Manuals	Records Management	Calendars/Planning Notebooks	Time Management/Goal Setting	Project Management	Event/Meeting Planning	Space Planning	Recycling Systems	Kitchen Design/Organizing	Closet Design/Organizing	Garage Design/Organizing
Martin, Patricia 415-749-0399				●	●	●	●		●	●	●	●	●	●		●	●	●
Mathis, Ellen P. 310-433-6509				●	●	●	●		●		●	●				●	●	●
McArthur, Susan 415-388-4950			●	●		●	●	●				●						
Merriman, M.Ed., Elizabeth 415-383-3318				●		●	●				●	●						
Metz, Katherine 415-348-7822				●	●									●				
Miller, Kerry 415-751-6619			●	●	●	●	●	●	●	●	●	●		●	●		●	
Myrrha, Anacaria 415-454-9343				●		●	●		●	●				●				
Newsom, Olinda G. 415-321-7525					●									●		●		
O'Connor, Candice 408-477-9027				●	●		●							●		●	●	●
Pauker, Gloria 818-886-6830	●			●	●					●	●							
Plakun, Scott 415-955-0506										●	●	●						
Poer, Kathleen 415-382-1218				●	●									●	●	●	●	●
Pollar, Odette 510-763-8482				●		●	●		●	●								

Garage/Estate Sales	Pack/Move/Relocate	Books/Libraries	Memorabilia/Photographs	Packrats/Chronic Disorganization	Errands/Personal Shopping	Seminars/Training	Speaking	Writing/Publishing	Manufacturer/Supplier	Alameda	Contra Costa	Marin	Mendocino	Napa	Sacramento	San Francisco	San Mateo	Santa Clara	Santa Cruz	Solano	Sonoma	Other
●	●	●	●	●	●	●	●			●	●	●				●	●					
			●			●																Greater Long Beach Area
												●										
						●	●			●	●	●	●	●	●	●	●	●	●	●	●	Phone coaching Nationwide
	●					●	●			●	●	●	●	●	●	●	●	●	●	●	●	Travel worldwide
	●					●	●			●	●	●				●				●		
						●	●	●		●		●				●						
																	●					Palo Alto
	●		●	●												●		●	●			Monterey Co.
		●		●		●	●	●														Los Angeles area
						●	●	●		●	●	●	●	●	●	●	●	●	●	●	●	Bay Area and beyond
						●	●		●	●	●	●			●	●	●	●		●	●	
	●					●	●	●		●	●	●				●						Travel Nationwide

SFBA CHAPTER / NATIONAL ASSOCIATION OF PROFESSIONAL ORGANIZERS DIRECTORY OF MEMBERS	Services																	
	Accounting/Bookkeeping/Financial	Health Insurance Claims	Computer Consulting/Training	Office Organizing	Residential Organizing	Paperflow/Workflow Systems	Filing Systems	Procedures Manuals	Records Management	Calendars/Planning Notebooks	Time Management/Goal Setting	Project Management	Event/Meeting Planning	Space Planning	Recycling Systems	Kitchen Design/Organizing	Closet Design/Organizing	Garage Design/Organizing
Prince, Terry 916-684-1401				•		•	•				•	•				•	•	
Raleigh, Barbara 408-732-0740				•	•	•	•	•				•		•		•	•	
Read, Claudia 303-755-7867				•	•	•	•			•	•		•					
Reis, Karen S. 408-720-1069																		
Ricks, Allison 510-614-0770				•	•	•	•		•			•	•	•			•	•
Roethe, T. J. 510-937-0396				•	•					•	•		•	•		•	•	
Rohrbach, Annie 415-461-3537				•	•	•							•	•		•	•	•
Rossow, Mary E. 415-969-4939				•	•	•	•				•	•	•	•	•			
Rossum, Karen M. 408-688-2550				•		•	•			•	•							
Sacks, MBA, Lynn Mortimer, 714-722-1225				•	•	•					•			•				
Sagal, Jan 916-885-4701				•		•	•		•	•	•			•				

Garage/Estate Sales	Pack/Move/Relocate	Books/Libraries	Memorabilia/Photographs	Packrats/Chronic Disorganization	Errands/Personal Shopping	Seminars/Training	Speaking	Writing/Publishing	Manufacturer/Supplier	Alameda	Contra Costa	Marin	Mendocino	Napa	Sacramento	San Francisco	San Mateo	Santa Clara	Santa Cruz	Solano	Sonoma	Other
		•	•			•	•	•														San Joaquin County
•	•	•				•	•											•				
								•		•	•					•						Denver, CO
			•															•				
	•	•	•		•					•	•					•	•					
					•	•	•			•	•				•	•			•			
•	•	•			•					•	•	•				•						L.A. & Orange Co. & travel for relocations
	•				•	•	•			•	•	•	•	•	•	•	•	•	•	•	•	Midwest Office, Natl, International
																	•	•	•			
	•				•	•	•															Orange & Los Angeles Co., Nationwide
					•						•					•	•					Placer, El Dorado, Monterey Co.

SFBA CHAPTER — Services

NATIONAL ASSOCIATION OF PROFESSIONAL ORGANIZERS — DIRECTORY OF MEMBERS

Member	Accounting/Bookkeeping/Financial	Health Insurance Claims	Computer Consulting/Training	Office Organizing	Residential Organizing	Paperflow/Workflow Systems	Filing Systems	Procedures Manuals	Records Management	Calendars/Planning Notebooks	Time Management/Goal Setting	Project Management	Event/Meeting Planning	Space Planning	Recycling Systems	Kitchen Design/Organizing	Closet Design/Organizing	Garage Design/Organizing
Saunders, Suzanne O. 415-456-4-SOS				•	•	•	•			•	•		•			•	•	•
Schechter, Harriet 619-581-1241				•	•	•	•				•							
Schomp, Gretchen 415-381-0129		•	•	•	•	•	•	•		•	•			•			•	•
Schwartz, Zoe 415-332-8688					•													
Scordino, JoAnn M. 415-474-9140				•	•	•	•		•			•	•	•	•	•	•	•
Shankle, Susan 415-574-2301				•	•	•	•		•						•			
Skibitzke, Judy 415-694-7979				•	•							•		•		•	•	•
Smith, Jeanne K. 415-493-3948	•	•		•					•		•		•					
Stanford, Alice 415-883-1104				•	•	•	•			•	•			•		•	•	•
Stelter, Sandy 707-426-3729			•	•		•			•			•						•
Stephens, Patrick 916-927-4869	•			•	•	•	•	•	•			•	•	•				
Stivers, Jane 916-966-0889				•	•		•											
Strassman, Frances 510-339-7474				•	•	•	•	•		•	•			•		•	•	•

	Provided										Counties or Areas Served												Other
	Garage/Estate Sales	Pack/Move/Relocate	Books/Libraries	Memorabilia/Photographs	Packrats/Chronic Disorganization	Errands/Personal Shopping	Seminars/Training	Speaking	Writing/Publishing	Manufacturer/Supplier	Alameda	Contra Costa	Marin	Mendocino	Napa	Sacramento	San Francisco	San Mateo	Santa Clara	Santa Cruz	Solano	Sonoma	
						•							•				•						
							•	•	•													•	San Diego & Orange Co.
				•							•	•	•		•		•					•	
											•	•	•	•	•	•	•	•	•	•	•	•	
		•		•				•			•	•	•	•	•	•	•	•	•	•	•	•	West and East Coast
									•									•	•				
		•																•	•				
	•	•				•	•	•									•	•	•	•			Estate Organization
		•			•	•					•	•	•	•	•		•	•		•		•	Los Angeles and Colorado
			•		•	•						•				•					•		
						•	•	•			•	•				•					•		
			•	•												•							
			•				•	•	•		•	•	•				•						

SFBA CHAPTER

NATIONAL ASSOCIATION OF PROFESSIONAL ORGANIZERS

DIRECTORY OF MEMBERS

Name	Accounting/Bookkeeping/Financial	Health Insurance Claims	Computer Consulting/Training	Office Organizing	Residential Organizing	Paperflow/Workflow Systems	Filing Systems	Procedures Manuals	Records Management	Calendars/Planning Notebooks	Time Management/Goal Setting	Project Management	Event/Meeting Planning	Space Planning	Recycling Systems	Kitchen Design/Organizing	Closet Design/Organizing	Garage Design/Organizing
Strauss, MA, RCA, Carolyn 310-841-2330	•			•	•	•	•					•	•	•		•	•	•
Streich, Dorothy I. 707-255-9509				•		•	•	•			•	•	•					
Sutherland, Georgia L. 408-446-1612				•	•			•				•	•			•	•	•
Thomson, Judy 510-793-6828		•	•	•	•	•	•	•	•	•	•	•	•	•				
Tom, Janet 415-864-5487	•			•	•	•	•	•	•	•								
Turitto, Kathleen 209-474-2186						•	•	•				•						
Vander Lans, Nancy 415-324-2031				•	•	•	•		•			•		•				
Velasquez, Sherri C. 707-552-0760				•	•					•	•		•		•	•	•	•
Voorsanger, June 415-922-8296				•	•		•		•				•					
Wallace, Angela F. 415-383-8387					•		•		•			•	•	•				
Watkins, Sharron 916-259-3310	•	•		•	•	•	•	•	•		•						•	
Wegenast, Carol 415-365-8804				•	•	•	•			•	•	•	•	•		•	•	•
Westcott, Arleen 415-751-2166				•	•	•	•			•	•	•		•	•	•	•	

Garage/Estate Sales	Pack/Move/Relocate	Books/Libraries	Memorabilia/Photographs	Packrats/Chronic Disorganization	Errands/Personal Shopping	Seminars/Training	Speaking	Writing/Publishing	Manufacturer/Supplier	Alameda	Contra Costa	Marin	Mendocino	Napa	Sacramento	San Francisco	San Mateo	Santa Clara	Santa Cruz	Solano	Sonoma	Other
			•	•		•																Los Angeles County, International
														•						•	•	
	•		•			•		•	•						•		•	•	•			
	•	•	•							•	•					•	•	•				
	•	•	•	•						•		•				•						New York & London
							•															San Joaquin County
	•	•	•	•	•					•	•	•				•	•	•	•			
•	•					•	•	•							•	•				•	•	
																•						
						•	•			•	•	•				•					•	Other areas by arrangement
•				•																		Plumas & Lassen Co.
•			•	•	•	•	•											•	•			
	•				•					•		•				•	•					

FLEXADDRESS®

LIFETIME ADDRESS BOOKS

Always current and perfectly organized, FlexAddress LifeTime Address Books combine the personal style of the traditional written directory with the organizational benefits usually reserved for a portable electronic organizer.

Through the quick-change magic of the patented FlexApeel® Insert Pages, simply peel away old, outdated entries and replace them with new ones over and over again.

Every LifeTime Address Book features a complete set of FlexApeel Insert Pages and Dividers designed for all your initial entries and many more.

For more information or to order, call

1-800-221-0431

Customized
Planning Notebook
Systems

by

Personal Resource
Systems, Inc.

P.O. Box 2529, Del Mar, CA 92014
1-800-255-9018
Fax 619-259-1624

Day Runner, Inc.

2750 West Moore Ave., Fullerton, CA 92633
1-800-232-9786
Fax 714-680-3487

To obtain additional copies of this book, complete the form below and send it with your check or money order to:

The San Francisco Bay Area Chapter
National Association of Professional Organizers
1592 Union Street, Suite 721
San Francisco, CA 94123
(Allow 4 to 6 weeks for delivery)

Please send me ___ copies of *Organizing Options: Solutions from Professional Organizers* @ $14.95* per copy (California residents add sales tax). Add $3.00 shipping and handling for first copy, plus $1.00 each additional copy.

Please type or print neatly.

Name _____

Address _____

City_____ State _____ Zip _____

Telephone (_____)_____
In case we have questions about your order.

*To inquire about discount rates for multiple orders over 10 copies, call 415-281-5681.

Notes

Notes

Notes

Notes

Notes

Notes

Notes

Notes

Notes

Notes